PRAISE FOR

The Contemplative Mom

"Ann Kroeker has captured the intense thrill and deep satisfaction of living life in loving, intimate relationship with our Lord Jesus Christ. And she doesn't want to tell you about it—she wants to take you by the hand and pull you along into your own unique quest with God that will help you cope with your daily challenges while bringing balance and fulfillment to a satisfying and rewarding life."

—VONETTE Z. BRIGHT, cofounder of Campus Crusade for Christ

"Contemplative? Mom? The words don't go together. But they should. This book gives busy, loving, kid-centered mothers permission to rest, like a tired child, in God's strong arms. An important book."

—RACHAEL AND LARRY CRABB, authors, speakers, parents, and grandparents

"Ann Kroeker offers realistic ways in which the resources of God's kingdom, in the grace of our Lord Jesus Christ, can be abundantly available to a mom where she is and flow from her to her children. This book shows us how the most powerful spiritual practices of Christ's people through the ages are available to moms today."

—DALLAS WILLARD, author of numerous books including *The Divine Conspiracy* and *Renovation of the Heart*

"If you're a pooped-out mom and need some practical tips for igniting intimacy in your relationship with God, this is for you. As you are laying down your life for your children, Kroeker will lead you step by step into the life-changing presence of the One who gave His life for you."

—PAM VREDEVELT, author of *Espresso for Your Spirit, Espresso for a Woman's Spirit,* and *Empty Arms*

"This unique and extraordinary book can change your life. Ann Kroeker's words are profound, deep, lasting, and exciting. Her concepts are inspiring, her ability to stimulate reader involvement remarkable. In the swooshing, noisy, whirling carousel of motherhood, Kroeker's invitation to live an inner 'quietness with God' causes the spirit to soar to a holy vow. Amidst dirty laundry and screaming babies, the reader's heart can vault to a determination to follow in Kroeker's steps and become a unique 'contemplative mom' to her own children."

—RUTH VAUGHN, author of 39 books, including *Who Will I Be for the Rest of My Life?* (coauthored with Anita Higman)

"So many people fear that the season of parenting is a barrier to spiritual growth. Ann Kroeker understands that it is a season filled with its own unique opportunities and challenges, and she gives wise, practical guidelines to use along the way."

—JOHN ORTBERG, teaching pastor at Willow Creek Community Church and author of *The Life You've Always Wanted* and *If You Want to Walk on Water, You've Got to Get Out of the Boat* the contemplative mom

the contemplative mom

Restoring Rich Relationship

with God in the

Midst of Motherhood

Ann Kroeker

SHAW

WATERBROOK
PRESS

The Contemplative Mom
A SHAW BOOK
Published by WaterBrook Press
2375 Telstar Drive, Suite 160
Colorado Springs, Colorado 80920
A division of Random House, Inc.

ISBN 0-87788-122-7

Library of Congress Cataloging-in-Publication Data
Kroeker, Ann S., 1967-
    The contemplative mom : restoring rich relationship with God in the midst of motherhood / Ann S. Kroeker.
        p. cm.
    Includes bibliographical references.
    ISBN 0-87788-122-7 (pbk.)
        1. Mothers—Religious life. 2. Motherhood—Religious aspects—Christianity. I. Title.

BV4529.18 K76 2000
248.8'431—dc21

                                                                                                00-037382

Printed in the United States of America
2002

10 9 8 7 6 5 4 3 2

To Philippe, Isabelle, Sophie, and Nathalie

Contents

Foreword

Ann Kroeker's book is fast paced, to the point, and brimming with encouragement for women in the crunch years of child rearing who crave a more intimate relationship with God but don't know where to start in pursuing it. The book would be worth the money just for the suggested reading list at the end, but there's so much more: Scripture verses selected to highlight the loving desire God has for us, practical hints for carving precious moments of solitude out of chaotic days, ideas for turning those moments into oases of spiritual refreshment, and insightful comments from other moms.

If there's anything that mothers of all ages—and everyone else, for that matter—need as we move into the complex world of the twenty-first century, it is a passionate, empowering, grounding relationship with God. That is the relationship to which *The Contemplative Mom* calls us.

—LYNNE HYBELS
Willow Creek Community Church
coauthor with Bill Hybels of
Fit to Be Tied and *Rediscovering Church*

This book is not a theological treatise. It is not a textbook on the spiritual disciplines or an all-inclusive encyclopedic resource. I doubt that's what you're looking for anyway.

This is more like a discussion with a friend. An encouragement. I'm writing as a peer in the trenches: a busy mom trying to figure out how to raise my children, love my husband, serve my friends and my church, and in the midst of it all—transcending it all—be a fully devoted child of God.

We moms don't give ourselves many contemplative, reflective moments. We're so busy serving others that a moment to ponder anything other than pizza versus tacos for dinner seems self-indulgent. But you're giving yourself a contemplative moment right now. You've chosen to read this book—or at least this page of this book. You're stepping out in faith that you might be able to live a contemplative life in the midst of motherhood.

I honor that. I believe it's possible. Although I am entirely in process, I believe God Himself has drawn me close to Him and shown me how to live a contemplative life, committed to Him, in the midst of motherhood.

And now your story and mine—your *hopes* and mine—intersect at this point in eternity. That is no small thing; I don't take it lightly. And I write with anticipation, knowing that both your life and mine will be forever changed because in a way, we will have met in these pages. That's how I feel when I read a book. I feel I have climbed into the mind, and often the heart, of an author.

I invite you to climb into my mind and heart and meet with me. These thoughts reflect how God has graciously worked in my life. I hope you realize that He is graciously working in yours. You're already responding to Him by moving toward a richer, deeper relationship with Him. I feel privileged to share in that.

May this book be a gift to you.

Acknowledgments

Much of the richness in my relationship with God is a direct result of how He has worked changes in me through my husband and our three children. This book is dedicated to them for the way God has blessed and taught me through our intertwined lives.

The fact that there is actually a book preserving my experience of God is a tribute to my husband, Philippe. This extraordinary man has supported me in every way: freeing up time for me to experience solitude and to write, suffering through late-night read-throughs, and tolerating—even encouraging—quirky contemplative experiments.

Isabelle, Sophie, and Nathalie have slept through most of my work hours, but they've experienced firsthand my contemplative life as I have tried by God's grace to live out the principles presented in these pages. We're all in this together.

My editor at Harold Shaw Publishers, Joan Guest, has believed in this project from day one and supported it with enthusiasm and confidence. Perhaps that's because she's a contemplative mom herself, inventing ways to deepen her relationship with God while editing manuscripts, relocating the Shaw offices, enduring an onslaught of e-mails on and around my deadlines, and still getting her kids to music lessons on time. *The Contemplative Mom* is in the hands of readers because of this talented woman. Thanks also to Barbara Hicks and Elisa Fryling, who handled all the last-minute work. They made this book stronger and clearer.

My thanks also to Kathryn Donovan Wiegand, who refers to herself as a "contemplative mom." Her essay called "Childrearing Interlude," published in *Finding God at Harvard*,[1] has helped me think through at a personal level the tension and paradox captured in this image.

By the end of the book you'll feel as if you know the contributing moms who allowed their hearts, habits, and lives to be exposed in the quotes at the end of each chapter. I admire these women and want to publicly thank them for their own ministry to the reader and for sacrificing chunks of time for interviews during some hectic seasons:

Linda Bannister, mother of three, 10-17 years old [all ages reflect age at the time of the interview]

Barb Beecher, mother of two, 30 and 33 years old

Julie Christensen, mother of one, 3 months old

Susan Clark, mother of two (with a third on the way), 2 and 8 years old

Debbie Driskell, mother of two, 15 and 17 years old

Susan Ginn, mother of three, 3-6 years old

Anita Hopper, mother of three, 23-31 years old (and grandmother of three)

Lynn House, mother of two, 1 and 2 years old

Lisa Miller, mother of two, 1 month and 18 months old

Susan Mowery, mother of three, 7-12 years old

Beth Pfister, mother of four, 7-12 years old

Trish Southard, mother of one, 3 years old

Sharon Stohler, mother of two, 4 and 6 years old

Ruth Van Reken, mother of three, 25-29 years old (and grandmother of two with a third on the way)

Sonya Waters, mother of three, 1-5 years old

Kathy Whitmore, mother of five, 13-22 years old

Rae Wilson, mother of six, 22-31 years old (and grandmother of one with another on the way)

Linda Znachko, mother of four, 4-13 years old

Some of my closest friends weren't quoted verbatim, but their words have saturated my heart and been woven throughout the text just because we are so intimately involved in each other's lives. They are an integral part of this book, even though you'll see their names printed only here. I'm indebted to these women; I hope they know what an impact they've made—and continue to make—on me. You ought to know who they are: Nichole Barber, Jenné Beecher, Ruth Vaughn, Sally Morgenthaler, Karen Todd, and Wendy Wishnowsky.

And to my childhood friend Angela Danner, who dreamed with me about writing since, oh, let's say sixth grade; and who waited patiently for me to write a book other than *The Medallion of Kilimanjaro*, which I scratched out on wide-ruled paper and bound together with bread-bag twist ties: I say thanks.

My friend Garry Poole instilled in me vision for ministry many moons ago as my college pastor. He saw potential in me as a leader and a writer. We ended up working together for many years on countless writing projects. As a result of his mentoring, I am a stronger communicator today. Thanks, Garry.

Grace Community Church in Noblesville, Indiana, has supported me and this writing project over the years in countless ways—I especially want to thank our pastor and friend, Dave Rodriguez, and his wife, Penny. Special thanks to the worship team at Grace, too, where creativity and contemplation miraculously merge during our time together. I am very much who I am today because of the time I spend with these people.

I was born into a print-loving home: my journalist-parents provided a rich literary environment, surrounding me with the printed word quite literally by lining nearly every inch of wall space with books of all types, including a big dose of classics. They taught me to read at a very young age and encouraged my ability to read newspaper headlines upside down (a skill that consistently amazed their friends). To this day the smell of bookstores and libraries, newsprint and fresh ink makes me feel very much at home. Lately my parents' investment in my writing life has been to baby-sit for my children as I approached deadlines. So I thank my parents, Lynn and Dick Hopper, who watched the children while I tapped away at the keyboard back home.

I also thank my in-laws, Bud and Char Kroeker—journalists, writers, editors, and publishers in their own right—who similarly helped when they were visiting from Belgium. In fact, I need to thank them for raising a man who feels equally at home surrounded by books as I do. Philippe, too, was brought up around printing presses and ink and doesn't seem to mind that a substantial chunk of our budget goes toward purchasing bookshelves—necessary to store the stacks of books I seem unable to resist.

And to everyone—family and friends—who lived with us through Philippe's heart surgery back in 1997 and were part of God's working in our lives: thank you. You walked with me—whether you knew it or not—as I pursued a contemplative path of richer, more intimate relationship with God through Jesus Christ. All of you who sent an e-mail or prayed or performed some generous act of mercy and service are part of this book too.

Chapter 1

Our Richest Relationship

Now this is eternal life: that they may know you, the only true God, and Jesus Christ, whom you have sent.

JOHN 17:3

Imagine the early days of a romance. Late-night phone calls, long walks hand-in-hand. Whispered secrets. Emotional electricity. Legs that turn to butter when you make eye contact across a crowded room. Remember the racing heartbeat, those adoring eyes…sweaty palms?

You don't remember? Oh, come on, think back…waaaay back. Ah, there. Now you're grinning. See, you *can* recall the sensations, pleasure, and delight, the inexpressible joy of being with your beloved, can't you?

Now, consider this: God wants this with you.

Okay, maybe He can't clasp hands with you or catch your eye across the room, but He longs for that inexpressible joy with you…the fresh thrill of enthusiastic love, the passion for His presence.

But He wants more than emotional thrills. He wants for us the fullness of love—a rich, deep love that builds over time. He wants us to know Him in a way we might equate with a healthy marriage. Through the years the love, trust, and the relationship itself intensify, grow rich and strong.

A SPIRITUAL PASSION

If you think of the different kinds of relationships between God and His people that Scripture describes—the marriage relationship, especially—this is not exaggerated, outlandish imagery. A spiritual consummation of this love, marked by passion and ultimate intimacy and union, is what He wants for us...*with* us.

What about other relationships? Jesus offered many metaphors to help us get our arms around a God we can worship in spirit and truth: Friend-to-friend, Father-to-child, Brother-to-sister, Master-to-servant, Savior-to-saved. Teacher-to-pupil, Leader-to-follower, Creator-to-creature.

Some of these metaphors, when we consider the depths of emotion they involve, seem almost unimaginable for a relationship between ourselves and God. Others seem comforting—sure and steady.

He is the God of the universe, the Creator of all living things. Yet He came to earth to be known more intimately than your most intimate relationships. As the Holy Spirit, He penetrates and inhabits us, knowing us more intimately than our husbands do. He gives good gifts as our loving, long-suffering Father. He teaches with patience and kindness as the Holy Spirit stirs us to action or change.

He wants a real, everyday, living, loving relationship with us that is both simple and complex: complex in that He is wild and free, with thoughts higher than our thoughts by the stretch of eternity; yet simple in that He wants to be the first thought of our day.

He is reaching out to us, and He wants us to reach out to Him too. He asks us to express the things that irritate us and to articulate the dreams stashed in our hearts. While He doesn't *need* us the same way we need Him, He *does* desire our love, attention, gazing eyes, tearful responses, and our companionship. We may delight in Him as He, likewise, delights in us, "For the LORD takes delight in his people" (Psalm 149:4).

Wistfully we long to move in step with the Lord, responding to all that we learn about Him. We wish for exclusive time with our Prince, our King, our Bridegroom. We want to be wholly devoted to the One who laid down His life for us. He stands by our side, defending us, like a supernatural knight in shining armor. He embodies relational ideals and surpasses them all. Oh, how we crave a depth of relationship with God beyond our wildest imagination! We look for time when we can pore over Scripture to gain insight into the One who loves us so intensely and powerfully…then we can engage in a riveting discussion and—no, wait!

There's this big glitch.

It's the whole "mom" thing.

Doggone it. If we were strictly "contemplatives," as we might picture a nun, let's say, then maybe we could easily foster this kind of intimacy with God. There would be so many advantages we don't have now: We'd slip on a symbolic ring to represent a marriage of sorts to the Lord Jesus Christ. We could live out the images we now merely dream of in our heads…dreams of uninterrupted prayer time, a thoughtful rhythm to our days, and traditions that emphasize His presence. In that scenario we *could* take long, meditative walks and pore over Scripture, getting to know our Beloved more than any other.

Someone else would ring the bell and we'd wake for morning prayer. We'd sing some psalms and have communion that *someone else* would serve. We'd sit down for a simple meal that we may or may not have helped make. We'd have the simplest wardrobe and own neither a curling iron nor hot rollers. We wouldn't have to worry about wall décor or cleaning the carpets, especially if we were shuffling around in some medieval abbey with stone floors. Ah, simplicity. We'd be contemplatives. Of course, we definitely would *not* be moms, given that whole vow-of-chastity thing.

But we are. We're moms. And as moms, *we* are the ones ringing the morning bell to get everyone else up. *We're* the ones fixing the meals and planning out the day's schedule—a schedule, I might add, based not on the religious calendar but driven more by soccer schedules, PTA meetings, and work hours. And our simple wardrobe is replaced by bulging closets packed with clothes for every occasion, complete with shoes and earrings to match.

This is the setting in which we must somehow achieve this kind of intimate, passionate love relationship with the Lord. These are our restrictions, our challenges. Is it idealistic to think it's possible to really know Him? A far-off dream? A fantasy? Or is there a slim chance that the concept of a "contemplative mom" is something other than the paradox it seems at first glance?

THE CONTEMPLATIVE PARADOX

With to-do lists longer than a roll of toilet paper, our chance at intimate prayer and exclusive times of reflection or study gets lost in the details of an average mom's day. Our "walk with God" feels less like a pleasant excursion with the Lord of love and more like a wretched assignment at the bottom of the list (if it made the list at all). We feel guilty if we don't make an effort, or we trudge through some kind of halfhearted devotional when and if we do make the effort. Or perhaps we want to be closer to God—we really want to—and just can't figure out how.

Because the Lord isn't bodily present, it's easy for Him to be forgotten, our thoughts of Him absently buried at the bottom of the laundry basket like a lost tube sock. We have plenty of flesh-and-blood relationships in our face to distract us from Him too. Depending on our stage of parenting, the so-called "flesh-and-blood" distractions either tug at our coat sleeves and demand cups of juice or they beg for keys to the car and a cell phone with voice mail.

Are we resigning ourselves to a puny, halfhearted, sidetracked relationship with God during the intense years of motherhood? What about the passion? The thrill? The goose bumps?

I can't guarantee goose bumps, but I propose that it *is* possible for *everyone* to restore a rich relationship with God. Yes, even busy women in the midst of motherhood.

Jesus calls us to be His disciples regardless of our life circumstances. He knows we have children to raise and households to manage. So it must be possible—with God all things are possible! Can we figure out *how* to interact with Him? Because frankly, my friend (and you must sense this too or you would have passed right by this book), we desperately need this intimacy with God to survive, to thrive, and to have anything worthwhile to pour into the people under our care and influence.

While this book can offer principles, it can't offer a step-by-step plan. Because you are unique, your adventure with the Lord will be unique as well. You will have to take the principles presented here and form your own plan, your own steps. As you trust Him, He will guide you down a contemplative path that seeks greater intimacy with Him while embracing and celebrating your unique calling in life as a mother.

Let's let go of our yearning for the pre-mom days of extensive study and quiet times. Sure, maybe it was easier then to find time alone. It was calmer then, with only our own and maybe our spouses' needs to consider. But now we're moms. The logistical challenges may be greater, but our actual relationship with Christ can be rich in different ways—and our time with Him certainly more appreciated.

Because we are mothers, we can understand aspects of the kingdom of God in ways non-moms never will. We live out parables daily that Christ can use to teach us if we open our hearts to Him. The Lord Jesus can open our eyes to see our daily circumstances the way He sees them. As we see, we will understand more about both ourselves and God Himself.

But it won't be easy. This book will offer many suggestions, but they are only starting points. Anticipate a unique experience with the Lord ahead of you, because you and He together make a relationship like none other since the beginning of time. My marriage has similarities to my friends' marriages, but it isn't a duplicate. Likewise, my relationship with God may be similar to yours, but it isn't the same. It can't be, because I'm not you. So you're going to have to let Him lead and guide you, conforming you gradually to the image of Christ.

I'd like to share a quote I read several months ago. It's from the pen of Phillips Brooks, the man who wrote the well-loved Christmas carol "O Little Town of Bethlehem." Even though it's a little stuffy in style, it grabbed me. Take a look:

> The great danger facing all of us…is not that we shall make an absolute failure of life, nor that we shall fall into outright viciousness, nor that we shall be terribly unhappy, nor that we shall feel [that] life has no meaning at all—not these things. The danger is that we may fail to perceive life's greatest meaning, fall short of its highest good, miss its deepest and most abiding happiness, be unable to tender the most needed service, be unconscious of life ablaze with the light of the Presence of God—and be content to have it so—that is the danger: that some day we may wake up and find that always we have been busy with husks and trappings of life and have really missed life itself. For life without God, to one who has known the richness and joy of life with Him, is unthinkable, impossible. That is what one prays one's friends may be spared—satisfaction with a life that falls short of the best, that has in it no tingle or thrill that comes from a friendship with the Father.[1]

Wow. There's some powerful, applicable stuff packed into that quote. Read it and you'll see that we're in danger. We moms are in danger of letting the husks and trappings of life—yes, the swim clubs, spilled milk, dirty dishes, piano lessons, and car maintenance—keep us so busy that we miss life itself, *real* life; that is, life in Christ.

I don't want to miss that. I want the tingle, the thrill, the richness and joy of life with the Father through Jesus Christ. I want intimate interaction from friendship with the Father. I want to be available to offer the most needed service, to be conscious of life ablaze with the light of the presence of God.

A life ablaze with the light of the presence of God. Yes. That's the target. I don't want to be just a soccer mom or the neighborhood's Kool-Aid mom. That's nice, of course, and those are great nurturing roles. But above all, I want my soul to be ablaze. I want to exude the light of the presence of God that shines from my rich relationship with Him—in the midst of motherhood. I pray we'll all be spared satisfaction with a life that falls short of the best and has no tingle or thrill that comes from a friendship with the Father.

The God of the universe wants to know us and be known by us. You are His friend, His beloved, His delight.

Is He yours?

EMBARKING ON THE ROAD TO RICH RELATIONSHIP

It takes practical steps to continue on the journey to a richer relationship with God. You might try some of the following ideas:

- Take a minute for informal self-analysis: Does a richer relationship with God seem unattainable? Do you feel you "ought" to be closer to Him, or do you long for the intimacy of a love relationship and just can't make it happen? What are you expecting out of this book? What are you expecting out of God? What are you expecting out of yourself? Talk with God about your answers.

- Start to see yourself as belonging to God: "I have been cruci-fied with Christ and I no longer live, but Christ lives in me" (Galatians 2:20). How does He want to live His life through you? Ask Him. When kingdom values begin to drive your life, much that frustrates you may fall into perspective.

- Set your watch timer to beep on the hour. Each morning, assign yourself an hourly response. Hear the beep and respond (internally or out loud) with something like "Lord, I love You," "You are my Beloved, and I am Yours," or "God is good all the time." Cluing in your children makes it a family affair ("Hey, kids! There goes my beeper—time to sing the Doxol-ogy!"), or you can keep it a personal, inner meditation moment as you silently express yourself ("Bless the Lord, O my soul" or "May the meditation of my heart be pleasing in Your sight, Lord").

- No energy? The mere thought of responding to a watch timer makes your stomach churn? If you feel mired down in the quagmire of motherhood, if you can't fathom how your rela-tionship with God can be richer, if you're intimidated, scared, or exhausted and you just want to give up…admit reality! This frees God to conform you to His image instead of your trying to smash yourself into His. Say, "Lord, I can't do this" or "Help!" God Himself lifts the burden from you and puts it on Himself. Let Him creatively guide you, showing you each step of the way how to walk closer to Him, *with* Him. If one thing doesn't work, that's okay. Just scrap it and try another sugges-tion. His mercies are new every morning. Maybe some of those mercies come to us in the form of ideas.

- Stash Bibles throughout your house or apartment and in your car. When you have a moment—and only a moment—you can conveniently access God's Word. Try one in the bathroom, by your bedroom mirror, in the kitchen, near the TV, next to the computer, on your nightstand.

- Start thinking of God as an ever-present loved One who wants to hear from us anytime—all the time! Practice a natural dialogue with God throughout your day.

- Inventory the activities in your life. Are your days out of control, filled with some things that you could say no to? Consider how you might slow the pace of your life by backing out of some responsibilities and building more space, more "margin," into your life. Then you can begin meeting with God and moving at a more reflective pace—at least every once in a while.

- Look for everyday clues that God loves you and is actively involved in the details of your life. Start a journal and record them, or write a one-sentence note in your daily planner or calendar. It will be a record of His handiwork to look back on. (It could be as simple as: "I read Psalm 42:1 this morning and then saw a deer cross US 40 while driving to work. I *want* to thirst for Him. When I saw the deer, I began to believe He is hearing my prayers.")

A Time to Reflect

Following are a number of Scripture verses. This is not a study, just a few verses to ponder. Nothing fancy. Depending on your time, look up one or two of the verses to get a context, and then think about them while you are going about your day. Use whatever time you have. You can "meditate" during snatches of time tucked into your day: while waiting for spaghetti water to boil, stuck in the carpool line, brushing your hair. Don't be overwhelmed by all these scriptures. Just pick one verse that jumps out at you and write it on a card to prop by your desk or sink or to stick in your jacket pocket. Think about it during the day.

Wonder about it. Ask God what He wants you to know about Him through it. "What does this mean in context? What does this mean to me? Is there something I should gain from this? Lord, please lead me here, because I'd love to hear from You."

He tends his flock like a shepherd: He gathers the lambs in his arms and carries them close to his heart; he gently leads those that have young. (Isaiah 40:11)

These commandments that I give you today are to be upon your hearts. Impress them on your children. (Deuteronomy 6:6-7)

A bruised reed he will not break, and a smoldering wick he will not snuff out. (Isaiah 42:3 and Matthew 12:20)

For nothing is impossible with God. (Luke 1:37)

Her children arise and call her blessed; her husband also, and he praises her: "Many women do noble things, but you surpass them all." (Proverbs 31:28-29)

From the lips of children and infants you have ordained praise because of your enemies, to silence the foe and the avenger. (Psalm 8:2)

[H]e who began a good work in you will carry it on to completion until the day of Christ Jesus. (Philippians 1:6)

[T]he fruit of the Spirit is love, joy, peace, patience, kindness, goodness, faithfulness, gentleness and self-control. (Galatians 5:22-23)

The LORD is my shepherd, I shall not be in want. He makes me lie down in green pastures, he leads me beside quiet waters, he restores my soul. (Psalm 23:1-3)

Cast your cares on the LORD and he will sustain you.
(Psalm 55:22)

See that you do not look down on one of these little ones.
For I tell you that their angels in heaven always see the face
of my Father in heaven. (Matthew 18:10-11)

Therefore, whoever humbles himself like this child is the
greatest in the kingdom of heaven. (Matthew 18:4)

And whoever welcomes a little child like this in my name
welcomes me. (Matthew 18:5)

Husband, Father, Friend

Compare the similarities and differences between your relationship
with God and your human relationships. What can we learn about
relating to God from the scriptures below?

Bridegroom-to-bride/Husband-to-wife
"For your Maker is your husband—the LORD Almighty is his name—
the Holy One of Israel is your Redeemer; he is called the God of all the
earth. The LORD will call you back as if you were a wife deserted and
distressed in spirit" (Isaiah 54:5-6).

"[A]s a bridegroom rejoices over his bride, so will your God rejoice over
you" (Isaiah 62:5).

Father-to-child
"For you did not receive a spirit that makes you a slave again to fear,
but you received the Spirit of sonship. And by him we cry, '*Abba,*
Father.' The Spirit himself testifies with our spirit that we are God's
children" (Romans 8:15-16).

"Because you are sons, God sent the Spirit of his Son into our hearts, the Spirit who calls out, '*Abba,* Father'" (Galatians 4:6).

"As a father has compassion on his children, so the LORD has compassion on those who fear him" (Psalm 103:13).

Friend-to-friend

"I no longer call you servants, because a servant does not know his master's business. Instead, I have called you friends, for everything that I learned from my Father I have made known to you" (John 15:15).

"The LORD would speak to Moses face to face, as a man speaks with his friend" (Exodus 33:11).

Brother-to-sister

"'Who are my mother and my brothers?' [Jesus] asked. Then he looked at those seated in a circle around him and said, 'Here are my mother and my brothers! Whoever does God's will is my brother and sister and mother'" (Mark 3:33-35).

"Both the one who makes men holy and those who are made holy are of the same family. So Jesus is not ashamed to call them brothers" (Hebrews 2:11).

Master-to-servant

"His master replied, 'Well done, good and faithful servant! You have been faithful with a few things; I will put you in charge of many things. Come and share your master's happiness!'" (Matthew 25:23).

"'I am the Lord's servant,' Mary answered. 'May it be to me as you have said'" (Luke 1:38).

"Whoever serves me must follow me; and where I am, my servant also will be. My Father will honor the one who serves me" (John 12:26).

"So you also, when you have done everything you were told to do, should say, 'We are unworthy servants; we have only done our duty'" (Luke 17:10).

Savior-to-saved

"For the Son of Man came to seek and to save what was lost" (Luke 19:10).

"For God did not send his Son into the world to condemn the world, but to save the world through him" (John 3:17).

"Believe in the Lord Jesus, and you will be saved—you and your household" (Acts 16:31).

"Therefore he is able to save completely those who come to God through him, because he always lives to intercede for them" (Hebrews 7:25).

Teacher-to-pupil

"Now that I, your Lord and Teacher, have washed your feet, you also should wash one another's feet" (John 13:14).

"Teach me, O LORD, to follow your decrees; then I will keep them to the end. Give me understanding, and I will keep your law and obey it with all my heart. Direct me in the path of your commands, for there I find delight" (Psalm 119:33-35).

"Teach me to do your will, for you are my God; may your good Spirit lead me on level ground" (Psalm 143:10).

Leader-to-follower

"[H]e leads me beside quiet waters" (Psalm 23:2).

"The man who enters by the gate is the shepherd of his sheep.... When he has brought out all his own, he goes on ahead of them, and his sheep follow him because they know his voice.... I am the gate for the sheep" (John 10:2,4,7).

"For the Lamb at the center of the throne will be their shepherd; he will lead them to springs of living water" (Revelation 7:17).

Creator-to-creature

"So God created man in his own image, in the image of God he created him; male and female he created them" (Genesis 1:27).

"For you created my inmost being; you knit me together in my mother's womb. I praise you because I am fearfully and wonderfully made; your works are wonderful, I know that full well. My frame was not hidden from you when I was made in the secret place. When I was woven together in the depths of the earth, your eyes saw my unformed body" (Psalm 139:13-16).

"So then, those who suffer according to God's will should commit themselves to their faithful Creator and continue to do good" (1 Peter 4:19).

"Through him all things were made; without him nothing was made that has been made" (John 1:3).

MOMS SPEAK OUT

It is so valuable to hear from moms who have gone before or who are in the trenches now. At the end of each chapter I'll relate parts of interviews I had with moms of different ages and backgrounds.

Barb: Being a mom is what drove me to the Lord over and over because I struggled so with feeling inadequate for the job. I became a believer when our children were very little. And it was in my home being a wife and mother that I learned so much about what it means to walk with the Lord and be a follower of Jesus. Being a mom is *really* where the rubber meets the road!

Sonya: Motherhood has boiled down my faith to the essentials. I'm so needy that if I don't have time in the Word for a week—which is not unusual—I'm desperate for it and I'm desperate for *Him.* It's not just this obligatory "do this because this is what I'm supposed to do," but it's because I'm broken about 30 percent of the time and I *need Him.* So it's very real. My relationship with Him has become more earthy and less defined since I became a mom. Like any relationship, you don't define it; you just live it.

Julie: God? God who? Okay, so that's a little extreme. I would probably characterize my relationship with God as "scattered and very limited." If I get fifteen minutes to spend any way I want, I am much more likely to read a novel than the Bible.

Susan M.: After I had my first child, I saw I couldn't have that quiet time every morning. I couldn't memorize these scriptures, and I really struggled for a long time because I thought, "I'm a terrible Christian because I'm not doing these things." So gradually I had to let go of that. One day I was reading about Moses, and I realized, "You know, Moses didn't even have a Bible! And look, he communed with God. You know, I *can* have this relationship with God apart from memorizing three verses a week."

Anita: I wish that I had been able to see the difference between the disciplines and an actual relationship with Christ. I was very good at having my quiet time and making personal applications *every time* I read the Word. If there wasn't something there, I'd *make there* be something! I was taught that the Bible is there to change our lives, and I believe it is—*it is!* But taken to an extreme, the disciplines take over. I'll go so far as to say that I had to stop the disciplines to begin to relate with God again. It just became something to check off. Something I was *doing*. You can become very comfortable, thinking, "Oh, I'm doing the Christian life." But I think eventually you're going to wake up and say, "Wait, who's God?"

Kathy: When you get on an airplane, they tell you what to do if there's an emergency, and they say that if the oxygen mask drops down you're supposed to put it on yourself first and then put it on the child beside you. When I first heard that, I thought, "That's so selfish! You should help the kid first!" Great, so you don't put yours on and help the kid instead, and halfway through you pass out and the kid's dead. This all goes back to the fact that if we aren't spiritually equipped, then we aren't going to be able to equip our children.

Anita: My dad got sick, and I had to spend about five or six months where all I did was go to the hospital every day all day long and watch him suffer. Everything else had to go. I had no physical energy to do anything but fall in bed for a few hours at night, then get up in the morning and do the same thing all over again. I felt like I had to keep my relationship with God stronger than ever because I'd never get through this if I didn't. So I thought *I* had to. Well, *I* couldn't. So what I did every day—out of sheer need—was when I took a shower I would stand in the shower and cry and say, "God, help me!" And that's all I could do. Eventually I realized that was enough. I think that is when I began to look at my relationship with God as a totally separate thing from "the disciplines" because I don't think God expected me to get up every morning and have an hour of quiet time at that point in my life. He knew. That's when I really began to see that I can have a relationship with God simply by doing the things that I have to do.

Barb: One of the most important things a mother can do for her children is help them understand that you are *there* for them, that they mustn't ever be afraid to "come home" and talk to you about *anything*. I guess there are two things that are essential in that process: One is realizing, understanding, believing, being convinced that my Lord is always there for *me*. I still remember the first time I saw Romans 8:38-39 and, through it, realized that *nothing,* no *thing,* could ever separate me from His love. It went down so deep in my heart that I believe that's what enabled me to pass on to my children that I will always love them, no matter what. Once you understand the Lord's agape love for you, it greatly enlarges your own capacity to love. The other essential factor is to listen, listen, listen. Again, understanding that the Lord always listens to me, I believe, helped me live out my ability to be a good listener. He has taught me the value of being a sounding board because He is my sounding board. Would I have demonstrated these characteristics without having the relationship I have with the Lord? Probably some, but not to the extent I did…and still do.

Chapter 2

Time Alone with the Beloved

And after He had sent the multitudes away, He went up to the mountain by Himself to pray; and when it was evening, He was there alone.

MATTHEW 14:23, NASB

Life in Christ is about relationship, and most quality relationships don't come easily. Most take a concerted effort to develop and grow. Rich relationships require time away from chores, commitments, and phone calls so we can spend time exclusively with the other, the beloved.

My husband and I struggle to schedule a date night with any regularity, but we eventually make it happen. These nights are essential for intimacy. Oh, for long stretches we can maintain a status quo relationship with the crumbs of conversation left over after draining days. But to build a rich and meaningful marriage that will dig into our souls and last a lifetime, we need more than crumbs; we need intimacy.

And frankly, it takes just as much time and effort—probably more—to develop intimacy with the Lord as it does with our spouse or anyone else. We can make do for long stretches, offering arrow-prayers on the run, but to build a meaningful relationship with the Lord, we need more. We need intimate time exclusively with Him, *the* Beloved.

We know this; it's just that…life happens. It rolls right over us, and somewhere along the line—possibly around the 124th dirty diaper—

we grow busy, preoccupied, and distant from God. And long after our youngest outgrows training pants, we look back and realize that we *stayed* busy, preoccupied and distant, not remembering that there was something more to our relationship with God. Or not believing that there *could be*.

When we do find a place and time to bare our souls to the Lord, the distance begins to melt away, and we experience Him at a level we might never have thought possible—especially if we've been satisfying ourselves with nothing more than a quick devotional thought before sprinting out the door.

God won't love us any more if we *do* manage to be alone with Him, of course, nor will He love us any less if we *don't*. Oh, no. He accepts us and loves us no matter what. This is not about earning His favor, nor is it about *doing*. This is about the relationship, not the sacrifices incurred while building the relationship. I may be emphasizing the effort needed to develop intimacy, but this is not about the effort. It's about *being*—being alone with the God who is longing to know us and be known by us.

SOLITUDE WITH GOD

We catch glimpses of God even when we're on the run, especially if we turn our thoughts to Him frequently. But it's hard to recognize His handiwork or hear His still, small voice if we don't periodically jump off life's proverbial treadmill or merry-go-round and slow down. Stop. Listen. *Be* with Him.

Times alone with the Lord train our ear to recognize His voice. Then when we're trapped on the treadmill or spinning wildly on that merry-go-round, He won't sound unfamiliar or distant. Drawing Him into our daily dilemmas will seem natural, an outgrowth of our foundational times alone with Him.

This stopping and listening is like a spiritual "date night." Some call it "solitude." When, how, and where it happens is up for discussion later in this chapter. But *that* it happens is key. If possible, we should aim to experience solitude regularly—and frequently—because the transformation to which the Lord is drawing us takes time. Preferably *concentrated* time so that we hear Him well and are able to respond.

You may be an introvert or extrovert. You may have twice as many kids as I do, or half. You may be married or single, work full-time, part-time, or stay at home as a family manager. Your kids may be school age or newborn. Your life may be simple enough that daily solitude will be an easy addition or so complex that you are on the verge of tears thinking about whether or not you'll be able to make time for it at all.

With so many possibilities, I can only offer principles and open-ended questions for your approach to solitude, leaving the rest up to you and God. I can't think this through with you individually, though I wish I could. I love to work through creative solutions and would relish the chance to see your face light up when God gives you an idea that might work.

Instead, you're going to have to pitch in and spend some time going through these suggestions with God's help. We need to ask Him for bonus creativity and courage to carve out the necessary time. Then, as we move into the later sections of this chapter, you are going to experience God for yourself in solitude.

NEVER ALONE

You may be primed for this kind of internal slowing, eagerly anticipating extended time alone with God. Or you may fear that you'll wave good-bye to the kids, arrive at your solitary place...and God won't show up. One friend of mine is such an extrovert she panics at the thought of pulling away from other human beings and busies herself with others to avoid being alone with God. Another is struggling with depression: Being alone is not her idea of a safe place. Those friends of mine—and you, too—need to know something:

You will not be alone. I can't promise *how* God will make Himself and His love for you known. He may *seem* as silent as ever. But He will be there. If it were possible, He would wrap His arms around you physically and assure you of His presence. You don't have to take my word for it either, because He says so Himself: "[S]urely I am with you always, to the very end of the age" (Matthew 28:20) and "I will never leave you nor forsake you" (Joshua 1:5; see also Deuteronomy 31:6,8 and Hebrews 13:5). Do not be afraid, He tells us.

"O LORD, you have searched me and you know me.... You discern my going out and my lying down; you are familiar with all my ways.... [Y]ou have laid your hand upon me.... Where can I go from your Spirit? Where can I flee from your presence? If I go up to the heavens, you are there; if I make my bed in the depths, you are there.... When I awake, I am still with you" (Psalm 139:1,3,5,7-8,18). You may feel you've made your bed in the depths and that God is far off. In these verses, though, He is assuring you that He is not a God who is far off. He is near, aware of your every move—not as a peeping Tom trying to pester and annoy you, but as a loving God who wants to reassure you that He surrounds you with His presence.

Over the years I've seen how *my* loving presence provides confidence for my daughters in many ways. For example, as each of them was learning to walk, I was right there, ready to catch or steady them while they stumbled along. The same thing happened when they were learning to swing or ride a bike.

Remembering how my presence provided my children with confidence lends insight into what God's own presence can provide for me: reassurance, protection, and confidence that I am His dear child and He surrounds me in every moment, helping me take bold steps forward or fall back into His arms. Always cling to the truth expressed through Paul in Romans 8:38-39: "neither death nor life, neither angels nor demons, neither the present nor the future, nor any powers, neither height nor depth, nor anything else in all creation, will be able to separate us from the love of God that is in Christ Jesus our Lord."

If that weren't enough, not only is His loving presence around you and with you, but if you are a believer in Jesus Christ, He is *in* you:

"My Father will love him, and we will come to him and make our home with him" (John 14:23).

"Do you not know that your body is a temple of the Holy Spirit, who is in you, whom you have received from God?" (1 Corinthians 6:19).

"I have been crucified with Christ and I no longer live, but Christ lives in me" (Galatians 2:20).

Believers in Christ are inhabited by the Holy Spirit. He makes His home in us. I can't say that I know exactly how that works, but there are verses galore singing its truth and mystery. This makes our time of solitude so intimate that no human relationship can compare. No one else literally inhabits us. God can ignite our souls as we recognize and embrace the truth—the reality—that He is in us and we are His.

I wish I could promise that if you dive into solitude with God you will always *feel* this love and *sense* His presence, but I can't. Wouldn't it be great, when you bring your struggles into your time alone with the Lord, if He would reveal some easy solution to your complicated emotional or psychological issues? He might. Then again, He might not.

Either way, I want you to know there is a safe place to be while you are "in process": in the presence of a loving God. He invites us to draw near to Him in our lumpy, unfinished, imperfect states. We don't need to have accomplished anything or overcome our weaknesses. We may have just yelled at the kids and kicked the dog.

No matter who you are, where you are, or what you're struggling with, the Lord Jesus Christ wants you to know beyond a shadow of a doubt that you are God's beloved daughter, in whom He is well pleased.

And He would very much like to meet with you.

MAKING TIME TO BE ALONE WITH GOD

Your first task is to find one substantial chunk of time—the longest you can manage—to spend alone with God. Just one, at least for now. Your first spiritual "date" is a one-shot deal that will pave the way for shorter, regular trysts in the future. A weekend would be fantastic, a day is great. Half a day is good, and an hour—well, we'll take what we can get.

Until recently, I had dropped all but a few extra-familial activities in order to live a slower, more reflective life daily, and even still the day was jam-packed with responsibilities and demands. Now, however, I have taken on more both at church and home and am probably only two commitments away from whizzing out of control. I underestimated how much time and energy motherhood takes. Friends with older children say it doesn't get any easier either. It's still hard, just different. So let's face it: Finding regular solitude is a challenge under any circumstances, but motherhood places particularly strenuous demands on a woman's shoulders.

Let's get ruthless though. To survive and thrive, time alone with God is a necessity. Can you slice one activity/responsibility completely out of your schedule just once? Maybe delegate something? The suggestions below may not be a perfect fit, but see if they spark another thought that will help you work within your own limitations. Later, you may be able to work one or two of these ideas into your weekly schedule, or maybe the Lord will give you other ideas for more regular solitude.

**Fifteen Tips for Making Time to Be Alone with God
(and Still Get Dinner on the Table)**

- Hire a sitter. Yes, it's perfectly acceptable to hire someone just so you can have solitude.

- Swap baby-sitting with a friend. It may be unrealistic financially to hire someone to watch your kids frequently, but try trading kid duties with a friend—you take her kids Wednesday afternoon, she takes yours Friday afternoon.

- Order pizza, and ask the family to eat without you one night (be sure to hand them paper plates). Where are you? Skipping dinner! Fast, and get alone with God.

- Put in a good video to occupy the kids, and leave the dishes. One time won't warp your kids or summon the health department. Even once a week wouldn't.

- Pack a sandwich, block off a lunch hour at work, and lock the door to your office if you have one. A "Do not disturb" sign should make things clear. Better yet, take off!

- Use your time on an exercise bike or treadmill at home or at the gym to pray. (Careful—someone might think you've fainted or slipped into a state of delirium and phone for medical help!) Or, for more freedom of expression, run or walk outside.

- Say no to the next thing that threatens to steal an hour of your week—even if it's a very good thing.

- Take a long bath and instead of letting your mind wander from loofah sponges to grout repair, choose to experience God.

- Announce a "quiet hour" in the house. Everyone to their rooms with only books and soft music. You, too. Instead of scrambling to do housework or reading a novel for personal rejuvenation, use this hour for God-centered solitude. (This is a great one to establish as a weekly ritual.)

- Turn off the TV.
- Request a vacation day, and dedicate it to a time of extended solitude. If you work from home, ask your spouse or a friend to request a vacation day and take over for you while you take off!
- If all else fails, grab solitude on the run: while waiting in the car to pick up a child or standing in line at the supermarket. You won't be able to lift your hands to the heavens, but at least you'll turn your mind to God.
- If your small children need monitored naptimes, lie down on their bedroom floor and, if they are quiet enough, direct your thoughts to God.
- Okay, maybe it's obvious, but...wake up an hour earlier or stay up an hour later.
- Continue asking God for ideas. He is a limitless problem solver and *the* Creative Genius. Don't underestimate His vested interest in helping you find time to be with Him.

If you honestly can't find one chunk of time to spend with God, flip ahead to some other chapters and let Him lead you through the suggestions listed there. If you feel loaded down with a pile of expectations, then you're missing the essential point of this book. Remember: *Relationship.*

At this point, then, I'll assume that you have blocked off the longest chunk of time you could find. Now let's actually step into solitude.

BEING ALONE WITH GOD

You are about to walk into an encounter with the living God. Your goal: simply to experience Him. This may or may not be one of your first experiences alone with the Lord. If it is, I'll walk you through it. If it isn't, I hope my suggestions will lead you to a fresh level of intimacy with Him.

You may find the slowing, sitting, and waiting uncomfortable and useless. You may be nervous or scared or wonder if you'll get bored. You may be anxious over what you're supposed to *do* or worry that you'll fall asleep in the middle of it. That's just fine. Be honest with yourself and God. I can't promise anything specific from this deliberate attempt to connect with God. All I guarantee is that Christ Jesus will be thrilled to have you all to Himself.

Grab your Bible, a notebook for journaling, a pen, and this book, and find a quiet, private place where you can cry if you need to—or shout, dance, or pound the floor with your fist.

If you sense that you need to write anything down throughout this time with Him, flip open your journal and scribble it out. You may find that a name comes to mind. A verse of Scripture. A situation. Whatever it is, record it. You may need to act on it later. In fact, keep a separate page or jot in the margins any distracting things that come to mind, like to-do-list items. Don't feel bad when these thoughts pop up. Just jot them down and move on.

Be aware that you may walk away from a time with God that you expected would bowl you over and end up feeling kind of *blah.* "All that trouble to get baby-sitting, rent a motel room, try to concentrate, and I get…nothing? Is this worth it?"

Part of the process is simply giving God the chance to speak on His time. Sometimes we wait to hear from Him. Sometimes there is what seems a silence from Him. Your time is not wasted. You may be waiting, but it can be an active wait. The spiritual sap inside of you may feel sluggish and lifeless, but seasons change. You'll eventually sense movement.

In a way this is God's time as much as it is our time. We can't dictate how He wants to spend it. We can simply be faithful to do what we feel He is asking. Don't forget, the holy God is with you. Right here. If you are a believer in Jesus Christ, He is always and forever in you—yes, *in* you—and He will never, ever leave you.

Explore as many or as few of the following ideas as you have time for. Some may resonate with you or give ideas for how you might naturally interact with the Lord. You might follow one suggestion down a track with Him that will take up all your time. That's fine too. There are no right or wrong steps. Right now, it's just you and God.

Now That I'm Alone with God, What Do I Do?

- Get settled. There's no perfect posture, per se, so do whatever feels comfortable or right. You might sit in a chair, on the floor, or even kneel if that seems appropriate. Take a deep breath and relax, especially if you've had a stressful time getting here.
- Ask the Lord to protect your mind and heart, your time…everything. Satan won't like the fact that you are about to interact with the King of kings. Let me pray for you too. "Lord, this is a holy moment, ordained by You, set apart for something amazing. This precious, beloved child of Yours is here, with You, willing to experience You however You lead. Please protect her from anything that might distract her or keep her from truly connecting with You. Move in and guide her; pour Your love into her. She's Yours. Help her to respond to You in faith and obedience. Help her truly encounter the living God. Through Jesus we pray, amen."
- Say something to the Lord about this moment, about how you're feeling or what you're thinking about your time with Him. Just talk to Him. It doesn't matter if it's out loud or silent.
- Thank the Lord for His presence. Believe He is with you.
- Tell the Lord some things you know are true about Him. Let Him know the positive things you feel about Him. Bless Him.

- If something is occupying your thoughts right now, tell Jesus about it.
- Describe the issues you're dealing with in your life right now.
- Overwhelmed? It's better to say, "I don't know what to do, Lord. I need You... Help!" than to try to figure everything out by yourself.
- Sit for a while without talking.
- Thank Him. Thank Him for spiritual blessings, like conviction of sin, forgiveness, eternal life, the Holy Spirit, and His tender love and care. Thank Him for relational blessings, your family, friends, church. Thank Him for material blessings, like the gift of a home, transportation, resources to buy food.
- Ask Him whom to pray for, and then interact with Him about each name that comes to mind.
- Is something holding you back? Ask God about it. Ask Him to bring it to the surface and help you get it out. He wants to help you.
- Be still for a while.
- Ask Him about your life, about future times of regular solitude with Him. Ask Him to show you what changes to make in your life, your schedule, your approach toward Him and your attitude.
- When pain shoots through you, pour out your heart. Everything—even the stuff you've never said out loud to anyone. The embarrassing things, the memories. This is your heavenly Father who already knows all of it anyway. You may have thought He wasn't there or didn't care. It's not true. I wish I knew the mystery of why He lets some terrible things carry on unchecked. But it isn't that He doesn't care. He passionately loves you. He has protected your soul. Let Him love you. Now. If you're angry, let Him know about it—even if you're angry

with Him. He can handle it. Follow this through, honestly exposing your heart. Ask Him for truth, for scriptures to lean on. Perhaps this: "I have told you these things, so that in me you may have peace. In this world you will have trouble. But take heart! I have overcome the world" (John 16:33).

WHEN YOUR MIND WANDERS

If you find yourself distracted during your time of solitude, try asking God for a piece of truth, whether it is one of the verses listed in this chapter, something you've memorized, or a statement about Him that is true. Henri Nouwen and others suggest using the "Jesus Prayer," which is based on the prayer of the tax collector in one of Jesus' parables (Luke 18:13). Just as the tax collector looked down and beat his breast as he humbly prayed, "God, have mercy on me, a sinner," the Jesus prayer beseeches Jesus, "Lord Jesus, have mercy on me, a sinner."

When you start to veer off mentally, say this prayer or another statement audibly or silently. Repeat it until you are all "here." If a particular scripture really grabs you—for either positive or negative reasons—look it up in your Bible and find it in context. Slooooowwww dooowwwnnn. Linger. Ask the Lord to "speak" to you personally. Maybe it stirs up a huge question. This is all good. Be honest. Stop when you sense God has something to say to you in a particular scripture. Live with the verse for a while. Sit still, and think about why He stopped you on that verse. (See chapter 5, part 2, for more detail on listening to God through Scripture.) If God brings to mind something to be confessed, admit it. Ask for His forgiveness and accept it. After pondering a verse, write out anything that seems appropriate: a prayer, your thoughts, your concerns, ideas He is giving you, another verse that pops to mind—some response to the word God has spoken.

- When joy floods through you, stomp on your inhibitions and fully express that joy. Be childlike and shout, sing, laugh, dance, jump up and down. For once just let loose and be free!
- Ask God for ideas about how to develop intimacy with Him.
- Ask Him to release you from the *do*ing mind-set. Ask Him to help you learn what it means just to be. Then, as much as He's shown you how, just *be*.
- Read some of the other chapters in this book, on such topics as communication and obedience. You will be led through suggestions for study and prayer that are perfect additions to a full day of solitude. Use them to continue building a rich relationship with the Lord.
- If you haven't written anything during this time, write a letter to God. Tell Him whatever is on your mind.
- If weather and time permit, take a walk outside.
- If your time is extended, have a simple meal, take a longer walk, do one or two replenishing activities. All of that is time with God too. Then have a second run at some of the other suggestions listed here.

A Time to Reflect

Read through the following list of Scripture verses. When a verse clicks with you, reread it, repeat it, and let it sink into your mind and heart.

Be still, and know that I am God. (Psalm 46:10)

He tends his flock like a shepherd: He gathers the lambs in his arms and carries them close to his heart; he gently leads those that have young. (Isaiah 40:11)

[A]nd when a prayer or plea is made by any of your people Israel—each one aware of his afflictions and pains, and spreading out his hands toward this temple—then hear from heaven, your dwelling place. Forgive, and deal with each man according to all he does, since you know his heart (for you alone know the hearts of men). (2 Chronicles 6:29-30)

Show me your ways, O LORD, teach me your paths; guide me in your truth and teach me, for you are God my Savior, and my hope is in you all day long. (Psalm 25:4-5)

How priceless is your unfailing love! Both high and low among men find refuge in the shadow of your wings. They feast on the abundance of your house; you give them drink from your river of delights. For with you is the fountain of life; in your light we see light. (Psalm 36:7-9)

The LORD confides in those who fear him; he makes his covenant known to them. (Psalm 25:14)

I will give you a new heart and put a new spirit in you; I will remove from you your heart of stone and give you a heart of flesh. (Ezekiel 36:26)

At that time Jesus said, "I praise you, Father, Lord of heaven and earth, because you have hidden these things from the wise and learned, and revealed them to little children. Yes, Father, for this was your good pleasure." (Matthew 11:25-26)

But when he, the Spirit of truth, comes, he will guide you into all truth. He will not speak on his own; he will speak only what he hears, and he will tell you what is yet to come. (John 16:13)

Search me, O God, and know my heart; test me and know my anxious thoughts. See if there is any offensive way in me, and lead me in the way everlasting. (Psalm 139:23-24)

[W]e speak of God's secret wisdom, a wisdom that has been hidden and that God destined for our glory before time began. None of the rulers of this age understood it, for if they had, they would not have crucified the Lord of glory. However, as it is written: "No eye has seen, no ear has heard, no mind has conceived what God has prepared for those who love him"—but God has revealed it to us by his Spirit. (1 Corinthians 2:7-10)

Set your minds on things above, not on earthly things. For you died, and your life is now hidden with Christ in God. When Christ, who is your life, appears, then you also will appear with him in glory. (Colossians 3:2-4)

This is the confidence we have in approaching God: that if we ask anything according to his will, he hears us. And if we know that he hears us—whatever we ask—we know that we have what we asked of him. (1 John 5:14-15)

SCHEDULING MORE TIME FOR GOD

You made it! You carved out time for a "spiritual date" with God. I hope it was wonderful. Would you like to spend more time with your Beloved? Perhaps on a regular basis? Maybe it's time to consider the next step in developing your relationship with God. It may be time to lop off one or two—or nineteen—of your responsibilities and pare down to the bare minimum. You will create more time for solitude, and out of that regular time with God, you may have all kinds of life revelations.

If you feel it's time to move on to this next step, you might reread "Fifteen Tips for Making Time to Be Alone with God" earlier in this chapter. Are there suggestions that you could use to carve out a regular time for solitude?

Another idea is to study a time-management book (see appendix for recommended reading). Use its suggestions to hone down your schedule and organize yourself to save time. You may have hidden pockets of time that will add up to what you need for solitude. Here are some freebies:

1. Have a plan for your day and your week. Don't just wake up and let life happen.
2. Write down *everything*. Keep a master to-do list, and transfer urgent and important items to your daily planner or calendar.
3. Keep only one calendar/notebook/planner that you carry everywhere.
4. Stick with one task until you're finished.
5. Organize your week in some logical way for taking care of the house. Perhaps a day for each major task (Monday is laundry day, Tuesday is grocery shopping, Wednesday is cleaning bathrooms, etc.).
6. Prioritize your to-do list by urgent, stressful, and important things. It helps get a handle on what *really* needs to get done.
7. Work solitude into that to-do list or as a regular part of your calendar. Soon it won't need to be carved out of other activities but will find a place all its own.

And once again—continue asking God for ideas. Remember that He is a limitless problem solver and *the* Creative Genius.

Moms Speak Out

The moms I talked to had a number of thoughts on their experiences and struggles with solitude.

Lisa: It feels so free to be so honest with the Father, even admitting when my mind is distracted. I found that has happened a lot; it's tiring to concentrate, especially when I'm just trying to listen and not say anything.

Ruth: For me, it's about *taking* time, not hoping for it. When my kids were small, I had a simple plan: Once they were in bed for the evening, I basically never, ever did my housework. I realize not all people can tolerate such a plan because their insides are more organized than mine, but that was 100 percent *my* time. I would read, I would study, but that's also when I spoke to God and listened for Him. Those were hard years in many ways, and these were the hours I would cry out to Him for understanding of why I couldn't be the person I had always hoped and wanted to be, as a mom, as a wife, and as His child.

Sharon: For so many years I was in a *do*-ing world, and really I'm a *be*-er. I'm *not* a *do*-er. So experiencing God by simply being His child is really freeing. I'm feeling comfortable with reflection and journaling and getting my thoughts out, realizing that it doesn't *have* to be anything profound.

Linda B.: When you have little kids, time alone is so hard to find. You need someone to help you find it, so I would encourage you to try to find someone to help you with that. I love to have a long quiet time— I like to have a solid hour. That's my favorite way to have a daily quiet time and to journal, but entire days are wonderful. The whole time doesn't have to be "spiritual" but can just be time alone to be creative or do whatever helps you be who you are.

Beth: Having your kids grow up is bittersweet. I miss those days when they were little and I was home a lot, but one of the perks now is that it is much easier to have quiet times. Even though it is absolutely insane driving kids from here to there every day, solitude is easier to come by.

Anita: I'd say the times I felt my relationship with God was richest and fullest was when my kids were smaller, when everyone says they have no time to spend with God. My husband really had to help me with this, but I used to take a day a week—a whole day—and I would go to a place where I could study. I studied the Scriptures and spent time in prayer. I think my life was somewhat simpler then. There were the demands of three small children, but it was all so contained. I think my world was smaller then.

Lisa: Why does my time with the Lord have to look the same on a daily basis? For instance, maybe a couple of days I can rise early. One evening I can retreat to my bedroom. Another day I can sit outside while Grace is napping. Part of the reason I get bogged down with the idea of "time with Christ" is that I've been brought up with a certain recipe: Get up early and read the Bible—no matter the cost (or how late you've been up the night before). I think the important thing is the relationship.

Anita: When my kids were junior high age, once a year I would take a little retreat by myself and spend two nights at a place like a state park. The first day I would go shopping, see art, do whatever I wanted to do. The second day I would spend the whole day with God. Not that I *wasn't* with God the first day, because I was always relating to Him as

I was looking at things, thinking and "contemplating." But the second day I was more in the Word and prayer. It took a husband who said, "Yes, I want you to do this." Actually I think a lot of husbands would probably do that, but *we* think we're too busy and our families couldn't possibly get along without us for two days. People have said, "But weren't you lonely?" *No!* It was honestly some of my richest times that I remember when my kids were younger.

Rae: When you have a baby that's been up since dawn and a five-year-old and so many distractions, it's easy to wonder, "How does the Lord fit into a busy schedule?" You might have to give up some things and make what seem to be sacrifices—like lunch with friends or whatever—but I want to say, "You give up nothing; you gain everything." The closer we grow to the Lord, the more our hearts conform to Him so that the desires of our hearts change: God in His incredible love and grace changes our desires. That is such an important truth. In the beginning, yes, you may feel like it is a discipline. Young moms who think that they have to spend time doing something else need to know that as you grow closer and closer to the Lord, He changes the desires of your heart. He conforms you more to Christ, and Christ's desire is to do the will of the Father.

Ruth: Solitude is that private interaction between God and me when I'm both talking to Him and listening for His answer. I pray, I listen, I hear, I record, I re-pray, I cry, I whatever. Although I usually do my Bible studies alone—I'm by myself when I'm studying—it's a bit different from what I would call true "solitude." Solitude, for me, is more that place of being just with God.

Chapter 3

Divine Companionship

[L]o, I am with you always, even to the end of the age.

MATTHEW 28:20, NASB

You hem me in—behind and before; you have laid your hand upon me.

PSALM 139:5

It used to be that when someone asked about my "walk with God," I'd cite how many minutes I spent in a recent quiet time or offer a quick overview of the latest Christian book I was reading. "How's your walk with God?" was shorthand for asking someone to describe her devotional habits in measurable ways.

But let's rethink that phrase, a "walk with God." Think of it as a literal walk: two people, companions, strolling together through life, perhaps hand in hand or one with an arm draped over the other's shoulder. Maybe they pause to carry on a more intense conversation, or they cross over to a park bench to sit for a while. I picture togetherness. Familiarity. Fondness.

Picture yourself on this walk with God. Ah, now it's much more than a one-liner from your verse-a-day calendar. It captures the beauty of our companionship with our loving Father and redeems the phrase, "a walk with God."

We long for this: someone to walk with us through life and hold us accountable. Someone to work side by side with us or just to sit comfortably in silence while we putter around in the kitchen. Can we really do this with the God of the universe? It seems silly to ask God to come and lean against the kitchen counter while we brush away the crumbs from our breakfast toast. That doesn't matter because we don't *have* to ask. He's already there.

Practicing the companionship of God in our hearts, minds, and souls can occur smack in the middle of a crowded subway, a health-food store, or a city park with kids squealing on the jungle gym. It can be achieved while soaking in the tub or jogging along Main Street. We direct our thoughts to the Lord and recognize the reality of His presence, care, and love.

Primed hearts can carry on a companionable dialogue at a stoplight or while folding clothes. Talk to Him about the moment or about some personal concern. Tell Him of your love for Him, or admit your confusion and doubt. In the middle of a mishap or dispute when you feel as if you're "losing it," ask Him to manifest the fruit of the Spirit in your words and actions.

BELOVED COMPANION

The Lord Jesus Christ is a constant companion. Our *ultimate* companion. As our ultimate companion, He is intimately interested in the details of our lives—not because He's particularly interested in toast crumbs or dirty socks, but because He is interested in *who we are.* He is interested in *us,* and crumbs and socks are a part of our lives, our realities.

God lovingly placed you on this earth and gave you new life in Christ in anticipation of relationship. You are His child, His friend, His beloved companion. He is passionately interested in everything about you: tasks, conversations, toothaches, and heartaches. He is ready and willing—eager, even—to relate to you on an everyday, personal level.

The problem I see most often in my own life is not that I need to be convinced of this truth, but that I need to be reminded of it—reminded of it so that I can act on it and consequently *inter*act with God. I suspect that most of us, while we're busy scraping dried pancake batter blobs off the kitchen counter, need to be reminded that Christ is with us. We don't forget the truth; we forget to *live* the truth.

That's me far too often. I know in my head and even in my heart that God is passionately interested in me, but practically speaking I forget. I forget to talk with Him about small matters, and then because I'm so out of sync with Him, I end up forgetting to bring even some of the large matters to Him. Why is it, for instance, that I grab the phone to call one of my friends when I have big news to share instead of interacting first with the always accessible Lord? He is a companion thrilled to hear my big news or to listen to my latest frustration or disappointment. What's more, He can offer supernatural assistance and empowerment. Most of my friends are helpful and sympathetic, but they can't empower me from within.

So when I neglect this interaction with God, *I'm* the one missing out. I'm missing out on this companionship, His power. I'm even missing out on a chance to learn from Him. As we interact with Him, rely on Him, and act on His requests—as we make ourselves available as conduits of His love and truth—we gain insight into puzzling or problematic situations. The fruit of the Spirit manifests itself more fully and frequently in our lives. Divine love makes us more Christlike—and makes us more effective parents. Why on earth would I want to miss out on all of that?

While I'm spooning applesauce onto my children's plates at lunch, God's divine presence is around and in me. When you cheer for your son at a swim meet or wait at the doctor's office, the Lord is with you and inside you. But how, during these moments, can we stay conscious of the reality of His loving presence? How can we avoid missing out on all God has to offer us? In short, how can we live in a state of divine companionship?

Well, it's a process; it takes time. And it takes effort to find ways to remind ourselves of the presence of God and look for the ways He reminds *us* of His presence. It will even take some effort to begin inviting Him to keep us company during our daily tasks—and accepting His moment-by-moment invitation to keep *Him* company.

REMINDING YOURSELF THAT GOD IS NEAR

One good way to build reminders of God's presence in our lives as a divine companion is to strategically place multisensory elements—items we can see, smell, taste, hear, or touch—where we are aware of them on a regular basis.

Churches have used multisensory "reminders of God" for centuries. Ancient cathedrals and church buildings were designed to engage people's imaginations and instill a sense of awe for God, compelling them to worship. Buttresses and ornate domes or steeples soared above people's heads, directing their eyes heavenward to encourage them to consider the transcendence of God. Stained glass windows visually told the stories that illiterate people weren't privileged to read themselves. Many churches still use incense and candles, artwork, crosses and crucifixes, communion, baptism—all multisensory elements in the environment and ceremony of worship.

What's to keep us from applying this principle in our homes? Are there multisensory elements you could work into your day or physically place in your home to remind you of Christ?

For example, think of something you could use to remind yourself when you wake up in the morning that God is with you. Do you need to scribble some scripture on a piece of cardboard to prop up on your nightstand? Would it work to buy a bathrobe or coat in a color that symbolically makes you think of Christ? As you pull it on, its color could awaken your sense of sight and touch to ground you in the truth that you are covered in the blood of Jesus (red), or serving the King of kings (purple), or robed in righteousness (white).

Or, perhaps, think of the shower stall as a confessional, and get honest with God about how you've blown it, how you've failed. Accept the spray of water as symbolic assurance that if we confess our sins, He is faithful and just and will forgive us our sins and purify us from all unrighteousness, washing us clean.

Could you incorporate new artwork or music into your home that compels you to worship Christ? How about switching to a new scented candle purposefully to surprise your sense of smell? You smell it…you note it's different…ah! That reminds you: God is present. The candle and its scent are meaningless except as they work to remind you of the all-present person of Christ. Even as I write, I have a bowl of scented oil on a cabinet. It's raspberry, a scent I've never used in my home before. I find myself catching a whiff, closing my eyes and smiling. It reminds me that God is here with me as I work.

God told the Israelites to teach their children His commandments and to write those commands "on the doorframes of your houses and on your gates" (Deuteronomy 6:9). Many of the suggestions below come close to fulfilling this command literally. Let these ideas inspire other ideas all your own to create a multisensory, God-honoring environment that reminds you of the reality of His presence and truth about Him.

Twenty-One Multisensory Reminders of God

- For a utilitarian approach, post a scripture on every mirror.
- For a more artistic version using Scripture, hire a friend who does calligraphy to create a flowing, beautiful version of a meaningful passage, and frame it as artwork in your home.

- For a ready-made version, buy a Timothy Botts book of expressive calligraphy. Maybe he's already done one of your favorite passages! Lay it open someplace strategic, or buy one of his posters to hang.

- Attach a plaque to your front door that reads something like "As for me and my house, we will serve the Lord." It will remind you of God's presence every time you enter. Or hang it at child's level to remind them, as well!

- Create a photo wall or tabletop display of friends and family as a reminder to pray for them—to interact with the ever-present God about their struggles or needs. (I call my display my "wailing wall" because so many of my friends face intense struggles.)

- Begin the habit of breaking your bread before eating it. No one needs to know that you are privately acknowledging and thanking God for His presence, His sacrifice, and His deep love for you.

- Set aside what you need for communion. If you feel comfortable serving yourself, put a bottle of grape juice and some crackers in the back of the fridge, and work in a moment during the day when you take it alone. Refer to *The Book of Common Prayer* (or similar reference) for prayers and Scripture.

- Create a personal "sanctuary" spot inside and/or outside the home, and place some reminders of God there, including a Bible and maybe a hymnal. You aren't "more" with God there than anywhere else, and He is certainly not embodied in any of those reminders. Pausing at this spot merely offers momentary solitude and can remind you of God's presence that is everywhere, all the time.

- Frame artwork that reminds you of God. You can order posters and large prints through Web sites and museums (see appendix), purchase a religious calendar and cut out the paintings you love most, or invest in a beautiful art book like one with Rembrandt's religious work. If you're brave enough and the thought doesn't make you queasy, use an X-Acto knife to slice out the pages you'd like to frame. (I bought some art books at a used-book store for a couple of dollars for this purpose, but the new ones are so expensive, you'll need to think long and hard before slicing!) Whenever you pass the framed art, pause and thank God for His presence. Our Creator God has given us beauty to enjoy and remind us of Him.

- Bring elements of nature into your home—start a pine cone, seashell, pressed flower, or leaf collection—or let a picture window frame living reminders of God: flowers, trees, cloudscapes, stars. "The heavens declare the glory of God; the skies proclaim the work of his hands. Day after day they pour forth speech; night after night they display knowledge" (Psalm 19:1-2). Let God's creation declare His majesty and remind you of His presence.

- Read to your child a Bible passage or story that is meaningful to you. Give him his choice of art medium, and ask him to sketch out or paint the story. Preserve and frame the finished work. You could include the Bible reference, print out a key verse from the passage, or let the art stand on its own.

- Research screen savers for artwork or icons that could flash a reminder for you at work. Or type out a scripture to flash on your screen saver "flying message" (where words scroll down and across the screen). Change it often.

- Invest in a wide range of sacred music, drawing from styles and eras that help you worship the Lord. Used-book stores or CD trade-in stores are good resources for music. Think outside your usual picks to keep the reminders fresh. Explore a variety of contemporary, ancient, and ethnic categories. Choosing something that is unexpected for you may increase its potential to engage your conscious mind.

- Observe silence for part of the day (when practical, of course —not when your guidance and input are crucial!). Minimizing exterior noise and your own phone calls, television, and radio background buzz reminds you that there is a reality in the not-heard.

- Own a talking bird? Train it to say, "He is alive!" or "Holy, holy, holy!" (Okay, okay, cut me some slack here. And don't go out and buy a bird just to do this!)

- To remind yourself of God's presence at key moments of shopping or bill paying, get checks printed with a background screen or watermark of Matthew 6:21: "For where your treasure is, there your heart will be also."

- Memorize and/or post in your closet Ephesians 4:22-24: "You were taught...to put off your old self...and to put on the new self." Anytime you change clothes, you can remind yourself of the fact that the old self is gone, and as you put on fresh clothes, praise God for the new self that through Christ Jesus has been put on. Applying makeup (isn't that practically like putting on a new self?) can also remind you to praise Him for making you a new creation in true righteousness and holiness.

- Memorize Colossians 3:12 about "clothing ourselves" with compassion, kindness, humility, gentleness, and patience. Then mentally "assign" various wardrobe and jewelry items that you wear daily to represent those inner qualities and to remind you that Christ is at work bringing them about in you. (Post the same scripture in your closet.)

- Use Deuteronomy 6:8 ("Tie them [God's commandments] as symbols on your hands and bind them on your foreheads") as inspiration for how you might have a scripture somewhere on your person, as a reminder. I've seen rings of all prices engraved with gorgeous Hebrew lettering. You could have an existing ring engraved on the inside with a Scripture reference important to you.

- Set an extra chair at the table to represent Christ's presence. Pull an empty stool into the kitchen while you prepare the meal. Imagine Him sitting with you.
- Change your fragrance if you wear perfume. Look for a name that seems appropriate, and let it remind you that you are to God the aroma of Christ (2 Corinthians 2:15).

Note that none of these things or experiences is to be worshiped for itself. Each idea suggested here, each item, is only a means to an

PRAYING THE DAY

Is it possible to plan your day in such a way that you create a new rhythm of life? Consider a monastic prayer cycle. This simple pattern is suggested by the Benedictines:

1. "Lauds" (morning prayer)—Meaning "to praise." This prayer is offered as soon after rising from sleep as possible. Sunrise equates with new light, new day, and Christ, our light, coming again.

2. "Sext" (noon prayer)—"Sext" is Latin for the sixth hour, which translates to our noon hour. This is an appropriate time to mark the middle of our day with the Lord and check in with Him.

3. "Vespers" (evening prayer)—Offered at sunset, before or after the evening meal. Give thanks for the day just lived.

4. "Compline" (night prayer)—Offered just before bed. Repent for sins and celebrate victory in Jesus.

end—a way to jar us into remembering God, acknowledging His presence, and worshiping Him as the Lord of the universe.

But do you see the basic idea? Consciously review the unique "signs" you already use in your environment to remind yourself of God, add some new ones, alter existing ones—and you will begin to notice a new rhythm in your relationship with Him.

Interact with God every single time you think of Him. Talk to Him on an ongoing basis—about small matters and about big requests. Remember that the items you place in your environment to remind yourself of His presence are to serve one purpose—that is, to inspire you to act. To remind you to talk with God: to pray, to worship Him, to thank Him for who He is. We may also gain something for ourselves—comfort, wisdom, and strength, for example. But any efforts we put forth to remind us that God is in us and around us are for this primary purpose: to compel us to adore and worship Him.

LOOKING FOR GOD'S REMINDERS

Another way to build our relationship with God is to be on the lookout for the ways He Himself reminds us of His presence—to notice the surprises He delights in giving us.

In her book *Pilgrim at Tinker Creek,* Annie Dillard writes about hiding pennies as a youngster for someone else to find:

> I would cradle [a penny] at the roots of a sycamore, say, or in
> a hole left by a chipped-off piece of sidewalk. Then I would
> take a piece of chalk and, starting at either end of the block,
> draw huge arrows leading up to the penny from both direc-
> tions. After I learned to write I labeled the arrows: SUR-
> PRISE AHEAD or MONEY THIS WAY. I was greatly
> excited during all this arrow-drawing, at the thought of the

first lucky passer-by.... The world is fairly studded and strewn with pennies cast broadside from a generous hand. But—and this is the point—who gets excited by a mere penny?... If you cultivate a healthy poverty and simplicity, so that finding a penny will literally make your day, then, since the world is in fact planted in pennies, you have with your poverty bought a lifetime of days.[1]

The world is planted in pennies "cast broadside from a generous hand." All around us there are clues that God is at work answering prayer, sparing us from something unpleasant or dangerous, teaching us something about Himself. Divine pennies gleam at our feet. How often do we step on them or ignore them in the busyness of life?

Start looking—really looking—at the world, at your life, at your

---

THE CHALLENGE OF FASTING

Fasting isn't easy for moms. We are the ones planning and shopping for the household's meals. Food prep is a big part of our job description; as soon as we've cleaned up from one meal, we have to mentally check if we have what we need for the next. Food is on our minds *a lot*. Still, if God calls us to this, what a tangible, physical reminder of our hunger and thirst for God! Pregnancies and nursing over the past eight years have kept me from serious fasting, but when I'm able, a friend and I fast one full day a week, scheduling a longer fast monthly. The accountability really helps. You could also fast from nonfood things: television, the computer and e-mail, anything that pulls you from God, away from a realization of His presence. *A Hunger for God,* by John Piper, is a motivating book to read as a primer on heart-motivations for fasting.

day. Examine it. Poke around, and see if God hasn't been hiding "pennies": hints of His active participation in your life and in this world. How much have we missed because we weren't looking?

You hear the laughter of your children in another room, for instance, and something registers in your brain. You make a connection: God is at work protecting those children and blessing your home with life and laughter.

Maybe you love sailing, and when you feel the spray of water on your face something stirs within you and connects you to the One who created it. Or you notice a red-tailed hawk soaring overhead or barely avoid a rear-end collision with a school bus or see your sullen teen smile for the first time in days. Something in each of these experiences somehow makes you aware of the presence of God. Pennies. Clues. Indications of God's deep love and involvement in our lives. Somehow the smaller things are evidence—promises—that He is at work in the big things.

My friend Ruth Vaughn wrote a book on this theme called *Letters Dropt from God*. In it she quoted a Walt Whitman poem:

> I see something of God each hour of the twenty-four, and each
> moment then,
> In the faces of men and women I see God, and in my own face in
> the glass,
> *I find letters from God dropt in the street,* and every one is sign'd by
> God's name.[2] (emphasis added)

Letters, pennies—whatever image you want to use for the evidence of God's handiwork in the world—are everywhere. They serve as reminders that God is at work, is omnipresent, loves us deeply, and is passionately and intimately involved in every detail of our lives. We just need to wake up and start seeing them, recognizing God's activity in our midst.

I've heard positive-thinking people like Oprah Winfrey suggest keeping a log, journal, or list of the things that happen each day that are positive—things they are thankful for. That's fine I suppose. My only concern for us is that if we keep a log like this, it should be much more than a list of positive things simply to help us feel better about our lives. Ours can be a log of God's loving commitment to us, of His involvement in our lives. It is a reminder list that He loves us and is pouring gifts out to us, however big or small they may be.

According to James 1:17, "Every good and perfect gift is from above, coming down from the Father of the heavenly lights." For our logbook, we can assume that the good things that happen in our lives can be directly attributed to our heavenly Father. We start looking for evidence and see it all around us: We land the much-hoped-for part-time job, or one of the closest parking spaces near the grocery store opens up on a rainy day. "Oh, that's a good gift. Thanks, God." When our teenager respects his curfew or someone sends anonymous flowers, we acknowledge the positive. "That's perfect. Surely God is doling out good gifts to me." And it's true! These things are great! By all means, grab your logbook and write them down. You're right, your heavenly Father loves you and wants to give you good and perfect gifts.

You might pull out a notebook, journal, or whatever you'd like to use to preserve these reminders from God each evening. Review your day for a few moments, and record the indisputably "good and perfect gifts" of each day.

Everyone's list will be different. You might include a word of encouragement from a spouse, friend, or coworker. Someone else might be jubilant about a "dry pants" day for her toddler in potty train-ing. Chronicle an answer to prayer or your surprise over a lower bill than expected for roof replacement.

On my list I could put this, for example: My friend Susan Ginn phoned me recently. Susan's husband faces serious health complications caused by a progressive form of multiple sclerosis. Many of their friends and I have been praying for God's mercy, and we've been looking for ways to help them out. Susan phoned yesterday to tell me that a mowing crew showed up at her house unannounced and proceeded to mow and trim her lawn.

"I'm standing at the window watching them, Ann!" she exclaimed. "I can't believe it! Now they're getting out the blowers and blowing all the clippings off our driveway! This is unbelievable!" To hear her delight at someone's surprise gift was an answer to *my* prayers for Susan. It goes on the log: "Mowers for Susan." That's all it needs to be. A reminder for me of the reminder from God that He loves me and He loves Susan. He's heard our prayers and wants to offer some good gifts.

Last night God also gave me insight into two areas where my older daughters needed encouragement. It was unexpected input. I was so grateful for the reminder. A good gift from my loving Father. A reminder that He's working in my life and in the lives of my daughters. These events or reminders may seem inconsequential to someone else. But we know, don't we? We know when they represent something significant. Start looking for God's reminders, and let yourself be surprised.

INVITING GOD TO KEEP YOU COMPANY

God is pleased anytime we invite Him to "keep us company," whether we're relaxing on the beach, shopping for carpet, or scraping burnt spaghetti sauce off the skillet. In fact, if you start to think of your errands and chores as acts of worship, you may be surprised; over time your tedious work may even begin to seem fun.

Work...fun? I'm someone who rushes (or else plods, martyrlike) through her tasks—especially the ones that never end, like laundry, dishes, and meal prep—in order to get *on* to the "fun." But the work itself? *I've* never considered it fun! Sometimes I play "beat the clock" to speed things up a little, but it doesn't make scrubbing the shower tile more *fun;* it just gets it over with faster.

Recently, though, I've been trying to see how I can make my tasks more enjoyable. Is there any intrinsic "fun-ness" to a particular chore? Or can I incorporate some fun into it—let's say through singing a song or making a game of it? Playing music in the background as I scrub the shower, for instance, does help get a rhythm going. It's a distraction for one thing, and sometimes for a few moments it marries with the task, and I feel a teeny tiny ray of hope: the possibility that there is something truly enjoyable about menial, mundane labor. Maybe if I work at it not only with my hands, but also with a sense of gratitude in my heart for the life God has given me, maybe then it would actually be fun.

When I started to think about it, I realized something else though: Working *with* someone who can interact with me while I'm doing my chores instantly makes the chores more fun. And then I realized that for most of my life I've had a perfect work companion available—and I've excluded Him! Yes, as crazy as it seems, when I'm scrubbing the toilet, God is there. When I separate the laundry, replace a light bulb, or put the groceries away, God is right there with me. What can I do to remind myself of that reality? Play worship music in the background, maybe? Sing a hymn? Pray out loud?

When we work at our tasks with all our hearts—when we recognize them as assignments from God and acknowledge His presence while we're doing them—we invite another level of companionship with Him. Even if we can't convince ourselves that our chores are "fun," we *can* dedicate them to God's glory.

In fact, with Christ as our companion, we have an opportunity as we perform our everyday chores to practice the servant leadership that is part of the process God uses to conform us to His image. The servant-leadership model that Jesus demonstrated as He washed the disciples' feet is one that we can practice every single day—as we literally scrub toes! With Christ beside us we can consider every pot washed, every pair of soccer shorts pretreated with stain remover, and every floor mopped as washed, pretreated, and mopped for Him.

Mother Teresa had some beautiful insights into this reality. We may not be serving the literally poorest of the poor in Calcutta, as she did, but her words are for us, too. "If you are really in love with Christ," she wrote, "no matter how small your work, it will be done better; it will be wholehearted. Your work will prove your love.... Whatever you do, even if you help somebody cross the road, you do it to Jesus. Even giving somebody a glass of water, you do it to Jesus. Such a simple little teaching, but it is more and more important."[3]

We may not think we are Mother Teresa's caliber, but all she did was love Jesus and do small things with great love. Our lives are similar to hers in that we are serving others all day long in small, simple ways. That is what He is asking us to do in our own homes, for Him, for the people He has given us to love for Him. Thus, all that we do we ultimately are doing for Him.

This makes our tasks lighter, beautiful, precious, and holy. "The simplicity of our life of contemplation makes us see the face of God in everything, everyone, and everywhere, all the time," explained Mother Teresa. "His hand in all happenings makes us do all that we do—whether we think, study, work, speak, eat, or take our rest—in Jesus, with Jesus, for Jesus and to Jesus, under the loving gaze of the Father, being totally available to Him in any form He may come to us."[4]

We are totally available to Him and His hand in all happenings. In Him we live and move and have our being. So, He is with us and we are with Him all the time, in every task, every chore.

The following poem, known as "The Divine Office of the Kitchen" or the "Kitchen Prayer," popped up on my e-mail through an automated "quote of the day" Web site. It summarizes well the idea of dedicating our everyday stuff to the Lord:

Lord of all pots and pans and things, since I've no time to be
A saint by doing lovely things, or watching late with Thee,
Or dreaming in the dawn-light, or storming Heaven's gates,
Make me a saint by getting meals and washing up the plates.

Although I must have Martha's hands, I have a Mary mind,
And when I black the boots and shoes, Thy sandals, Lord, I find.
I think of how they trod the earth, what time I scrub the floor:
Accept this meditation, Lord, I haven't time for more.

Warm all the kitchen with Thy love, and light it with Thy peace;
Forgive me all my worrying, and make my grumbling cease.
Thou who didst love to give men food, in room or by the sea,
Accept this service that I do—I do it unto Thee.[5]

How pleased God must be when we acknowledge His presence on a daily basis, when we invite Him to be a part of our everyday activities—when we can see our work as fun just because He's there with us, keeping us company.

It's not only in our tasks and chores, though, that we can invite Him to keep us company. What about during our "down" time? Why not enjoy a companion when we're jogging or when we're relaxing at the park watching the kids climb the jungle gym? Or when we're on our way to the movies? Hmmm. These days, it could provide excellent accountability to recognize that the Lord is with us in the theater, exposed to the same scenes and language we are. How about inviting God into our times of recreation? Or on vacation? He is, of course, with us anyway, but there is something relational and intimate about inviting Him along.

Sonya, one of the moms I quote at the end of the chapters, loves to hike in the mountains. She has told me details about idyllic hiking trips where she has, in essence, invited God to keep her company.

Interaction she had with Him about the smallest details of her journey yielded surprising encounters and revelations. While in the woods or mountains, crossing streams or stepping around hundreds of tiny frogs in her path, Sonya has experienced the companionship of God.

My friend Karen loves to work in the garden. Sometimes she just pulls the weeds and focuses on the task before her. But there are times when she is aware of His presence and, in a way, invites the Lord to join her in her relaxing times of planning and planting. Upon reflecting later, Karen has realized that she has gained remarkable insights into the kingdom of God directly related to gardening.

With the depth of relationship that's possible in our work and play and the fun we can enjoy with the Lord, why don't we do this more? Why, I wonder, do we so often live in poverty while the riches of heaven are available to us every moment of every day? What a loss when we don't enjoy the presence of God, and how disappointed God must be when we ignore the gift of His presence. The King of all kings sits, in essence, at our breakfast table, perfectly willing to take up an ongoing dialogue with us and be involved in the intimate struggles of our life. Fully available to provide us the strength we need to meet every challenge, the power we need to overcome sin.

Guess what? God hangs out with us not only because He can, but because He *wants to*. He doesn't get bored; He enjoys our company. And He's dedicated to our growth and our maturity in Him. He started a good work in you. He is faithful to continue that work. When He's perfected it, the experience you'll share with Him will be so deep and intimate we have no words to express it.

KEEPING GOD COMPANY

Imagine another culture, another time. A time of no post offices, no fax machines, no telephones or telegraphs, no Internet or e-mail—no technology of any kind. Imagine how relationships might have developed back then. Without the benefit of modern communications technology, how did people meet one another? Get to know one another? Deepen their relationships? Clearly, they had to meet face to face and spend time in one another's company.

Imagine, in that context, the significance of two people walking together. How would the experience have gone beyond what two people in modern times experience when they walk together? We enjoy intimacy in the company of a loved one, but in our culture we have many other ways of communicating. Is that an advantage? What if walking together was all we had to build a relationship on? Would it have drawbacks, or would it be an improvement on our instant-message world? What do you think a "walk with God" would have meant to someone in that earlier world?

I suspect that relationships where people spend a lot of "real" time together—literally walking together, working together, speaking directly to one another—boast the kind of companionship and comfort level we are looking for in our relationship with God. The Bible speaks of people who "walked with God." Could you imagine someone writing that—figuratively speaking—about you: "She really walks with God"?

A Time to Reflect

Read through the following scriptures—or even better, find them in your own Bible. (Note that italics throughout are mine.) Give some thought to the relationships described—and to the integrity and the capacity for intimacy of those persons said to have "walked with God." You might also read Psalm 23 with the idea of walking and being in the comforting presence of God, or read through Matthew, Mark, Luke, or John, and make note of the companionship Jesus and His disciples shared as He walked the earth. What does intimate companionship with God look like in our own world? How can we figuratively walk with God today?

> When Enoch had lived 65 years, he became the father of Methuselah. And after he became the father of Methuselah, Enoch *walked with God* 300 years and had other sons and daughters. Altogether, Enoch lived 365 years. Enoch *walked with God;* then he was no more, because God took him away. (Genesis 5:21-24)

> This is the account of Noah. Noah was a righteous man, blameless among the people of his time, and *he walked with God.* (Genesis 6:9)

> Blessed are those who have learned to acclaim you, who *walk in the light of your presence,* O LORD. (Psalm 89:15)

> Teach me your way, O LORD, and I will *walk in your truth;* give me an undivided heart, that I may fear your name. (Psalm 86:11)

> For you have delivered me from death and my feet from stumbling, that I may *walk before God* in the light of life. (Psalm 56:13)

> Whether you turn to the right or to the left, *your ears will hear a voice behind you,* saying, "This is the way; *walk* in it." (Isaiah 30:21)

> What agreement is there between the temple of God and idols? For we are the temple of the living God. As God has said: "*I will live with them and walk among them,* and I will be their God, and they will be my people." (2 Corinthians 6:16)

Whoever claims to live in him must *walk as Jesus did.* (1 John 2:6)

Yet you have a few people in Sardis who have not soiled their clothes. *They will walk with me, dressed in white, for they are worthy.* (Revelation 3:4)

MOMS SPEAK OUT

Linda: For me solitude sometimes is in the midst of noise. I try just to go into the kitchen by myself, and no matter what I'm doing, I try to be deliberately conscious of God. Our lives as moms are not quiet, but I still have the experience of God in the midst of that. We need to realize it *is* attainable. We *can* do that!

Julie: In some ways I seem to pray more often now that I'm a mom. They aren't long prayers, but they are more frequent. That's probably because I don't need two hands or a quiet room to be able to talk to God.

Susan G.: I'm glad our God is a God who is accessible twenty-four hours a day. I would die if I didn't have that access to Him. God tells us to pray without ceasing; to me that is so natural! I pray when I'm in the car. I pray when I'm in the shower. I pray when I'm in the middle of a struggle with my kids. I pray when I'm searching desperately for lost shoes when I need to walk out the door. I pray for lost keys *all* the time. I sit in the middle of the floor close to tears praying for help finding those keys. I pray constantly, and the Bible tells us to pray without ceasing. Our God has made it so easy for us to do that.

Susan M.: Having a relationship with God doesn't work by formula. It works by what I call "snippets and bits." It's catching things on the run. I carry a book or Bible in the car so that if I'm done with the carpool or working out and I don't want to go home yet, then I can just go sit in a parking lot and read my Bible for five minutes.

Lynn: I have a rich imagination, and sometimes I actually picture Jesus sitting on the swing next to me. I talk to Him while I swing. I make sure the neighbors are inside when I do this so they don't think I'm talking to myself. My prayers take on a sort of childlike tone as I fly up into the air.

Barb: I would dialogue often with the Lord as I went about my day, asking Him to calm me down, show me a better way of dealing with things, help me be more transparent and real, give me wisdom on how to handle a situation. I guess learning and practicing the principle of "praying about everything" is the key. Since I was such a worrier, it was a huge leap to learn that God was vitally interested in anything that was worrying me, big or small.

Linda Z.: If I sat down and prayed an hour and left that frame of mind, I wouldn't pray again all day. So in my mind I say, "I will pray all day," and I feel that I do a lot of the time. It's broken, yes, but in my car, with my kids, I try to make it a part of life.

Susan M.: When I swim, I try to come up with a verse for each lap. The first lap, maybe it's Psalm 1:1-2, "Blessed is the man [whose] delight is in the law of the LORD"; on up to lap 27, when I think, "All right! I'm on 27!" because Psalm 27 is one of my favorites; and so on until I get all the way up to 32, "Oh yeah, Psalm 32:5." So I end up going through all the Scripture I have memorized.

Linda Z.: There are things I can control to make my house quiet. For instance, I never watch TV during the day. I always cringe when I hear of young moms watching TV a lot.

Linda B.: As the years have gone by, the biggest thing that keeps coming back is prayer and learning that prayer is not just this time that you set aside. It's a constant thing. I tend to be a worrier. I'm certainly not there yet, but I think I have learned to process prayer in everyday things. When things start troubling me, I've learned to stop and just relax in God's love and realize that He does care about these things as much as I do. It's the whole idea of practicing the presence of God and turning it over to Him.

Trish: I put a verse in a candy dish in my refrigerator. It's verse 26 from 1 Corinthians 10: "The earth is the Lord's, and everything in it." I open the fridge, and I might enjoy a piece of something, but that verse stays with me. I even say it out loud sometimes, and my daughter Sabrina hears it, and now she's getting the hang of it. She associates it with candy, unfortunately, but she's getting it.

Lisa: Time spent with the Lord can look different every day. After all, it's different with my husband, Joe. I don't just give him an hour every day and only that hour at only that time of day. Part of what keeps the spark in our relationship is that there is variety to the time we're together. Sometimes it's a joy just to sit with him while he's reading and I'm doing nothing or working on dishes.

Chapter 4

Talking to God

Trust in him at all times, O people; pour out your hearts to him, *for God is our refuge.*

When Philippe and I learned that we were expecting our first baby, we agreed to wait until after the first three months to tell anyone. Oh, was that hard! I could barely resist sharing the news with friends and family! I wanted to share the excitement and have my friends and family jump up and down with me, scream in my ear, laugh and talk about all the big questions: "When's the baby due? Boy or girl? What will you name her?" Why was that so hard? Because when any human gets big news, people usually pop to mind—people we're dying to tell! "Phone Mom!" "Call Sonya!" "Bud and Char must know!"

The thing is—and I'll bet by now you can guess what I'm going to say—the Lord wants us to act on that first impulse by starting with Him. Is He first on our list of people we're dying to tell?

WAITING TO HEAR

Our knee-jerk reaction if we are moving toward a deeper, richer relationship with God should be "I can't wait to talk with the Lord about this!" And the good news is, we don't have to wait. And we never have to try again later because of a busy signal! God already knows, of course. Everything. But He wants to hear it from us. Our spontaneous sharing with Him is one crucial aspect of being known.

It makes prayer much more than merely a prescribed activity at a particular time, scheduled in like so many events in our lives. Prayer can be that. In fact, sometimes it should be that, and I encourage you to look into other ideas for experiencing God through that kind of formal prayer (see appendix for suggested reading).

But what I'm talking about here is relational interaction. Communication. Talking. Unloading our hearts with Someone who loves us and listens. This very well may happen at a defined time of solitude, or it may happen spontaneously while we're trimming the hedge or dusting the mantel.

Communication with God is the avenue by which we reveal ourselves. In our times of solitude—and as we develop a sensitivity and awareness of His presence—we can pour out our hearts to Him. At the first news of a big event, or during a time when nothing makes sense, or in the midst of everyday struggles when we need His input or empowerment, we can utter honestly, "Lord, I'm about to lose my patience. Move in me, here. Save me from saying something I'll regret."

He wants to hear it. The Lord Jesus Christ wants to hear from you, every big and little event, every sorrow and every joy. He wants us to reveal ourselves to Him honestly and completely, good news and bad. He wants to be a refuge, a safe place for us to express every spontaneous reaction and our first, unedited thoughts—about anything and everything, from getting a promotion to seeing our child take his first steps. He wants us to come to Him as well—ideally, even before we go to the other precious people in our lives—when our hearts are weeping and raw.

This isn't to say that we go to God in place of telling our joys and sorrows to our friends. Sharing with our friends and family is a good thing. I hope and pray that we can all have relationships with others that reflect the tender strength and love of the body of Christ. He put people in our lives so that we can carry each other's burdens—so that we can weep with those who weep and know there will be someone to weep with us when we need them. If we go to people in place of going to God, though, we are limiting the depth of interaction we might otherwise have with Him. Building a rich relationship with the God of the universe requires that we grow increasingly comfortable interacting with Him.

When we fail to share our lives with God, I think we frustrate Him—or worse. Scripture indicates, for instance, that God grew disappointed and angry when the Israelites regularly forgot Him, complained, and neither asked for His help nor thanked Him for His blessings. And what about the ten lepers whom Jesus healed? Only one came back and thanked Him. You can almost hear the sadness in Jesus' voice when He asked, "Where are the other nine?" Our first reaction should be to race to the Lord with it all: our thanks, our aches, our joys.

That's the theory. Unfortunately, sometimes we forget. We forget God's omnipresence, we forget His passionate interest in us—we forget to run to Him. Surrounding ourselves with multisensory reminders like those mentioned in the last chapter, however, can help to jog our memory.

Other roadblocks, too, may keep us from going to God with the details of our lives. Relational distrust is one of the hardest to overcome.

WHERE DO WE PUT OUR TRUST?

Think about a person in your life you love and trust. Revealing your heart to him or her comes naturally most likely. You probably long to know what is going on inside him, and you also want to share yourself.

Sadly, most of us can also think about a person in our lives who has betrayed our trust. Someone we once loved, someone to whom we once poured out our hearts. The phrase "rich relationship" hardly pertains anymore, does it? It's painful even to think of him or her. You held out your heart to this person in love, with trust. It was an act of faith. When the trust was broken, retreat and protection were natural reactions. Sometimes a personal betrayal can pierce so deeply that it affects every relationship—including our relationship with God.

Extending our heart in trust to anyone, hoping that this person will care tenderly for it, is an act of faith. When we've been betrayed, the thought of engaging in an active and intimate dialogue with anyone— including the Lord—can feel like slapping our palm onto a hot stove burner. We assume we'll end up seared again, scarred for life. Is it any wonder some of us keep people at a distance? Should we be surprised that some of us stay distant from God, locking our souls up tight?

I know women who have been betrayed by people who lied to them for years over matters too personal to put in print. Trust has been blasted to bits, and where once these women were open, honest, and eager to interact with the people they were closest to, they now cringe emotionally, even with individuals they should be able to trust.

These women have found their way back to trusting God, though they still struggle to trust some people. I know a few other women, though, who can't trust God after feeling betrayed by people they trusted. Putting up emotional guards and walling off their hearts have become habitual, and even the promise of rich interaction with the living God cannot seem to break down their fears and inhibitions. Some make their way back to the Lord, some don't. Either way, it's sad that it has to be so hard. It's sad that betrayal is disturbingly commonplace.

I have not experienced betrayal of that magnitude, and so I tend to approach relationships with a degree of childlike naiveté and trust that has allowed me to stay close to people and intimate with God. Where are you? If your trust has been destroyed by unhappy circumstances, I pray that you will find trust again with God. If, on the other hand, trusting God comes easily to you, I pray that you will capitalize on that and enrich what you already have.

Please keep in mind an important principle: Thinking about your life won't necessarily help you to understand God better, but knowing the truth about God will surely help you to understand your life better. Before you decide that not even God can be trusted, read the following verses about His dependability and trustworthiness. Then you can base your decision on truth and not only on circumstance.

A Time to Reflect

The LORD is a refuge for the oppressed, a stronghold in times of trouble. Those who know your name will trust in you, for you, LORD, have never forsaken those who seek you. (Psalm 9:9-10)

The LORD is righteous in all his ways and loving toward all he has made. The LORD is near to all who call on him, to all who call on him in truth. (Psalm 145:17-18)

[M]y enemy will say, "I have overcome him," and my foes will rejoice when I fall. But I trust in your unfailing love. (Psalm 13:4-5)

In you our fathers put their trust; they trusted and you delivered them. They cried to you and were saved; in you they trusted and were not disappointed. (Psalm 22:4-5)

Do not put your trust in princes, in mortal men, who cannot save. When their spirit departs, they return to the ground; on that very day their plans come to nothing. Blessed is he whose help is the God of Jacob, whose hope is in the LORD his God,

the Maker of heaven and earth, the sea, and everything in them
—the LORD, who remains faithful forever. (Psalm 146:3-6)

The LORD is good, a refuge in times of trouble. He cares for
those who trust in him. (Nahum 1:7)

Do not let your hearts be troubled. Trust in God; trust also
in me. (John 14:1)

May the God of hope fill you with all joy and peace as you
trust in him, so that you may overflow with hope by the
power of the Holy Spirit. (Romans 15:13)

The LORD within [Jerusalem] is righteous; he does no
wrong. Morning by morning he dispenses his justice, and
every new day he does not fail. (Zephaniah 3:5)

And when Daniel was lifted from the den, no wound was found
on him, because he had trusted in his God. (Daniel 6:23)

Yet this I call to mind and therefore I have hope: Because of
the LORD's great love we are not consumed, for his compas-
sions never fail. They are new every morning; great is your
faithfulness. (Lamentations 3:21-23)

The LORD himself goes before you and will be with you; he
will never leave you nor forsake you. Do not be afraid; do
not be discouraged. (Deuteronomy 31:8)

Trust in him at all times, O people; pour out your hearts to
him, for God is our refuge. (Psalm 62:8)

These verses only scratch the surface. Think of other key words or
phrases, and do a word study using a concordance. Look up *trust, faithful, long-suffering,* and *love,* and see what you can find out on your own.

You may have noticed from those verses the place where we can go for inspiration for developing intimacy with God, no matter how optimistic, naive, bitter, or confused we may be: Psalms.

The psalmists maintained intimacy, openness, and trust in God, even when they were clearly disappointed with or betrayed by people. All of us can use them as mentors as they model how to trust—even when trust doesn't come easily.

Read their unabashed expressions of lament, hope, joy, frustration, anger, and angst. They confess and repent. They sing with jubilant praise. They hold out their hearts in utter trust and faith that God will never injure, ridicule, ignore, or blast them. And He won't.

The psalmists poured out their hearts to Him, knowing that this kind of honesty led to the depth of relationship they yearned for. David seemed to grasp this most dramatically and expressed the widest range of emotions. But all the writers exude the passion of artists, expressing the depths of their hearts and souls. We can too.

Let's look to some psalms, then, as models for expressing total honesty. Psalm 51, for example, preserves David's response after Nathan revealed David's adultery with Bathsheba. This psalm models a broken and contrite heart, confession, repentance, and a plea to be restored and changed: "Restore to me the joy of your salvation and grant me a willing spirit, to sustain me" (verse 12).

Other psalms offer us similar truths in the midst of heartache. Look up Psalm 13, and you'll see a shift from pain and questions to trust in God's love, as David sings because of God's goodness. In Psalm 119:28 we hear of someone whose "soul is weary with sorrow" and who asks God to strengthen him "according to your word." Then in verse 32 he writes, "I run in the path of your commands, for you have set my heart free." The dichotomy of a soul weary with sorrow, yet a heart set free. Emotions. Honesty. Real life.

These are only three examples of the 150 models you can peruse in Psalms. Read through them in a consecutive loop, pondering one or two a day over the course of several months. You will be reassured as you see laid bare every emotion you struggle with daily. Look to the psalms for inspiration.

It is okay to hurt, you know. Part of the curse of living in this fallen world is pain and disappointment. Loss. But the sovereign God who transcends this world offers a safe place—a refuge—to retreat to. Even if you don't trust people, God Himself can be trusted. He hears. He acts on our prayers. He loves us and responds to us. He will never, ever betray us.

Take the risk—and the advice—of Psalm 62:8: Pour out your heart to God. For in pouring out your heart, you reveal yourself humble, broken, and open…letting yourself be known to the living God.

POURING OUT YOUR HEART TO GOD

We all have our own ways of communicating, ways that feel most natural and comfortable to us. As my friends will tell you, I love personal, one-on-one, face-to-face conversations. But when I really need to pour out my heart to God—when I'm not even sure what I want to say, but I know I need to say something—writing down my thoughts and feelings helps me express my heart more than anything. In fact, sometimes I think I would shrivel up if I didn't have access to paper and pen or my computer!

Not everyone feels the same, of course. You may be more comfortable talking to God out loud or taking a walk and praying silently or even putting your words to impromptu music. But even if writing doesn't come naturally to you, I urge you to give it a try. You may discover that journaling—writing letters to God, if you will—can help you communicate intimately with Him, freeing you to unload your heart fully. If you'd like to try communicating with God in writing but you're one of those reluctant journalers, the following practical tips may help you get started.

Journaling for the Faint of Pen

- Consider your personality: Are you a loose-leaf-and-three-ring-binder kind of gal? Leather-bound-blank-book? Wide-ruled-spiral-bound-at-eighty-cents-each? A fun picture on the cover may be so appealing you find it irresistible. Opening a notebook that seems "right" can eliminate awkwardness right away. (See appendix for blank book/journal resources.) Sometimes investing less allows more spontaneity and freedom to write big and scribble in frustration without feeling that you've ruined a fifteen-dollar book. Consider going cheap.

- Choose your pen or pencil carefully too, maximizing freedom of expression. You think I'm joking? Hey, just try it. Try a cheap ballpoint, then a Waterman fountain pen. See if one doesn't "feel" better than the other. Your mood may dictate a particular medium too. On the other hand, in moments of desperate need I've been known to snatch those minipencils at the library and scribble down my heart on a series of three-by-three-inch scraps of paper. Just because you left your journal and preferred pen at home, don't feel you're stuck. (I've pasted those scraps into the "official" book later!)

- Try an electronic journal. I know it may seem sort of cold and modern and not at all earthy. It's just that I use a little bit of everything. With an e-journal, I can practically keep up with my thoughts in "real time." When I really need to purge and my computer is available, I usually hop right on and spew it out. Try it—maybe you'll find you've just needed a faster way to get your thoughts out.

- Assume no one will ever read it. Ever. Otherwise you float around in "editor" mode, wondering how something sounds or rewriting sentences you think your mom might frown at. Write fast, keep your pen moving, and try to capture your "first thoughts," those first, instinctive, unedited thoughts. Don't think; just write. Often you pass through brain-edit mode and dip down closer to your heart. That's where real prayer happens.

- Follow threads that come up. You never know if your Aunt Lucy's name came to your mind for a deeper reason than expected. Be willing to give up control of what the journal should be filled with, and trust God to guide you.

- A more organized approach could include sections, perhaps in a three-ring binder. One section for prayer requests/concerns, another for sermon notes, another for Bible study. Then the journal is an extension of other pursuits of God. If I were trying this, I might go ahead and include a section of blank pages to record all those distracting to-do list items that threaten the integrity of my conversation with God.

- There is no right or wrong journal. Yours is yours. Maybe you'll want to paste in photos and make it more like a scrap-book. Maybe you'll have nothing but run-ons or sentence fragments. Who cares? This is between you and God. And the beauty of a journal is you can look back and see how God transforms you over time. You might like a weekly brain dump or prefer preserving a few small thoughts daily. Or switch around for variety!

- Organize your journals. This is one thing I regret not having done. Trying to figure out the chronology of a decade's worth of journals illustrates my superb lack of foresight. It's hard to look back and find things. Take my advice and put in the extra effort so you can look back. (Just assign a spot in your closet and stick the completed journals up there in order, or put them in a box in the basement marked clearly on the journals themselves and on the box.) One reason to stay organized is because your thoughts and responses can be easily accessed to share with friends. If your struggles in the past parallel with someone else's in the present, just look back and pull from your honest prayers. Share what isn't too intimate or embarrassing, and God may use it to transform someone else's life.

Journaling Distractions

One important note about journaling: Don't fret over mental distractions. Instead, do something about them! Some ideas that might help:

1. "Write through" the distractions. That is, write down the actual distraction as part of the text. "And Lord, I can't help thinking about the project I have to finish for Women's Ministry, and I need You to help me know what to do with that. If there's an idea I need to write down, please tell me. If not, help me focus on You because this is Your time."

2. Keep a separate list. I keep a scrap of paper to the side or write in the margins to-do list items, names of people to call. Just write them down, and deal with them later.

3. If it isn't something that needs to be recorded or acted upon, just imagine tying it to a helium balloon and letting it float away. Let go of it. Ask God to keep you attentive to Him.

4. Have a phrase from Scripture you can write down each time the distraction comes to mind. This would be a similar idea to use if you are meditating. Just transfer the idea onto paper.

- Journals can include multiple disciplines in addition to prayer communication or the outpouring of your heart. They can certainly incorporate study and note taking during sermons, for instance. You can be as organized as you like, or let your notes be imbedded with your prayers as a continuous flow.

MOMS SPEAK OUT

Susan M.: For me, pouring out my heart to the Lord is usually in the form of tears and is usually equated with some sort of physical posturing. In those moments I get an overwhelming feeling that I just have to get down on my knees. I stop what I'm doing. It's happened in the car, and I've pulled over. It's interesting to think of it as "pouring out my heart to God." If I started thinking about it that way more, it would probably increase my prayer life.

Susan C.: I believe "crying out" to God is in many ways the purest, most honest time of prayer for me. Without forethought, ceremony, or even expectations, my very human heart falls trustingly into the arms of my Father, and out tumbles my joy or my pain, a cascade of emotion and utmost vulnerability.

Sharon: Shame is one thing that keeps me from going to God. I recently identified something that had been going on in my thought life that went unconfessed. Even though I've known forever that God knows all my thoughts, my human nature makes me want to hide, hoping God won't notice my sin. How can I possibly pursue God passionately when I'm sure He'll "find me out"? The freeing and wonderful thing about it is He still loves me, even if I have to share things with Him that I'm ashamed of.

Susan G.: I'm facing the possibility of my husband's death to MS, and I'm definitely facing my husband losing his job in the near future due to his symptoms. When I pray to God or when I look to Him, it might not be a literal prayer—more of a lifting my eyes to the hills. When I'm thinking about all the things going on in my life right now, including my husband's illness, I think of it as submitting my fears to God. It takes a tremendous amount of faith, but it brings a tremendous amount of release to know that God will take care of me. Even if my husband dies, my God is going to supply my every need. I sit at His feet and think about what is happening, and I can't help but feel secure.

Susan C.: I have literally been facedown on the floor, weeping, questioning as I cried out to God; I have jumped into the air yelping for joy as I cried out to God. At the core of all this emotion is a very basic, miraculous reconnecting as I open my heart to the One who crafted it at the start to be filled by Him.

Barb: One of the worst times in my life was when my husband, Ron, died. The girls were fourteen and seventeen. I feared Ron's death would have such a devastating impact on their lives that they would always suffer because of it, be "scarred for life," and I would not be able to help them get through it. That overwhelming, fearful thought hit me so hard one afternoon about three weeks after Ron's death that I plopped down in a chair in my bedroom and cried out to the Lord, "I can't do this. I don't know how to survive myself. How can I possibly teach my girls how to get through this?" In that moment God reminded me that I was fully equipped because of my relationship with Him, that I already knew the "how." It's a moment-by-moment walk with Him— the same principle as Psalm 32:8, walking in the Spirit, letting Him guide and lead me. He reminded me that I wasn't alone in this. He was there and always would be.

Anita: I wish that I would spend more time in prayer, but I find it very hard to pray right now. I find it very difficult even to think that God is hearing me. And so I have short bursts of prayer, where I beg God to show me Himself, to show me who He is in the midst of this chaos of life, to hang on to me, and not to let me let go of Him. I want to be one of those strong people who never gives up…. I don't necessarily think He expects me to be strong. I think He expects me to be the mess that I am. I think what He probably wants is for me to be honest and just to be seeking.

Listening to God

Give ear and come to me; hear me, that your soul may live.

Isaiah 55:3

How precious to me are your thoughts, O God!

Psalm 139:17

Our profession of worship and our confessions of sin aren't flying into
outer space or dissipating into thin air. When we pour out our hearts
to Him, our heavenly Father hears us—every groan, every whisper,
even our unarticulated pain—and He responds by pouring out His
own heart to us. He calms our fears, challenges us, expresses His love.
When we learn to listen, He is there: teaching, encouraging, convicting. Changing us.

I think sometimes we worry that listening to God requires large
chunks of our time. Life doesn't always permit us to take those chunks,
however. What's more, we don't *need* to wait for a time of solitude to
hear from our Lord. He is speaking all the time. If we would take more
brief moments of time in the midst of our busy days—pause more
often from the clamor of dinner preparation or the din of traffic or the
noise of our morning routine—perhaps we'd hear Him. Stop. Turn off
the radio. Pause periodically and listen for the Lord.

I mean a literal pause. It's quite simple, really: while you're reaching for a pan in the lower cabinet, balanced on one knee and clanging around for the lid, just stop. Stop the clatter and pause. Breathe out a small confession, perhaps, and breathe in God's forgiveness and grace. (My gratitude to Campus Crusade for Christ founder Dr. Bill Bright for his concept of "spiritual breathing.")

A pause during any activity can be a listening moment. You might even work in a visual clue. Decide that at every stoplight, for instance, you will take an inner pause as well as a driving pause to check in with God: "Have I been drowning you out, Lord?"

Even when I don't work in a pause, however, I find that motherhood gives me an advantage as far as hearing God—sometimes when I'd really rather not listen! Children can be unexpectedly perceptive:

"Mama, why did you say that Mrs. Hamilton was weird?"

"You sure look different without makeup, Mom."

"Mom, why did you ignore that man's question?"

Gulp. Our children can be as effective as a healthy conscience, can't they? Sometimes I feel I hear from God through them. At least He often uses what they say to convict me or challenge me. Younger children, speaking in all innocence, spotlight our sin; older children often see our blind spots better than we do. A wonderful side benefit of their insightful (if not always welcome!) contributions: You can use your shortcomings to teach them about the universality of sin and the need for a Savior; you can model confession as you talk through your choices—especially your failures—with them.

THE EYES OF YOUR HEART

The Lord speaks to us in many other ways: Through trusted, godly friends and leaders, for instance. Through quotes from messages and sermons. Through answered prayer. He's often used authors in my life as long-distance mentors, teachers, and advisors. A passage from a book written by a godly man or woman might hold just the message I need for a particular moment or problem.

Music and art help me listen to God on an emotional level that I have a hard time reaching on my own. The first time I listened to Christian musician Chris Rice's album *Past the Edges* one of the songs caught me off guard. I was alone in the house when I heard "Missing You," a song about missing Jesus and clinging to His promise to return. I felt a flood of emotion: a longing to be with Jesus—to see Him, to touch Him…in person. Even though He's with me always, I missed Him. When will I touch Him, be held by Him, look into His eyes? It was as if the entire song was mine, an intimate expression of my deepest desire to be united with Christ Jesus.

"And though I know You're right here with me/Tell me when can I be there with You?" Rice writes.[1] Longing and emotion were stored up inside me, and God used Rice's lyrics to unleash them. I often stifle tears, but that evening I wept. I wept because I missed Jesus. I wept for joy, too, because by the end of the song I knew He was communicating with me and reassuring me of His love and presence. I sensed it with a force I hadn't for a long time. I prayed and listened to that song until I memorized the lyrics and could sing along with it over and over, until the sun went down and the kids came tumbling in the door with Philippe.

Henri Nouwen was moved even more significantly when he studied Rembrandt's painting *The Return of the Prodigal Son*. Seeing a reproduction catapulted him on a long spiritual adventure prompted by what was, in essence, visual "listening." Nouwen wrote an entire book on his experience. Try it for yourself. Find an inspiring print that depicts a Bible story. Live with it for a while. See it with the eyes of your heart. Listen to what God says through it.

In the next two chapters, we'll discuss in more depth other ways God speaks to us, particularly through impressions and through nature.

Maybe you can remember a time when you sensed the Lord wanted you to *do* something, something specific—when you felt a distinct impression that He was guiding you. Perhaps you've heard Him speak to you through nature; many parables await the discerning eye. Begin paying more attention to these and noting them. As you do, you may be surprised at how many different ways God communicates with us...and what He is saying!

Of all the ways we might hear God, I am convinced that the most reliable and dynamic approach to knowing what He thinks and wants—to knowing who He is—is His written Word. Go to Scripture often. Assume God has something to say to you. Listen. Listening is not a science, by the way. It's not really an art either. It's just two people trying to understand each other. Know each other. Communicate.

I've been confounded by enough misunderstandings to know that communication isn't easy. With *anyone*. Don't worry when communicating with our unseen God is a challenge. It *is* hard, sometimes, to know when we're hearing His voice. Again, let me encourage you to go to Scripture. Then measure every other word, every insight, every impression, against it. Always. No matter how convincing, anything that is contrary to God's revealed Truth is not from God.

GOD'S LOVE LETTER TO THE WORLD

Love letters. Written proof of the loved one's feelings. Ribbon-wrapped and preserved, read and reread, cherished for a lifetime.

A lover selects stationery that fits his mood, then he composes his thoughts and records them in ink with his best penmanship. He envisions his sweetheart's beauty as his pen swirls, forming the letters of her name. He drops his missive in a mailbox and pictures her eyes lighting up when she opens it. Then the days pass as he awaits a reply, wondering whether or not she accepts his profession of love.

The scene at the other end is just as lovely. She pulls out the mail, heart racing in anticipation. At a glance she recognizes his handwriting and shakes with excitement as she slits open the envelope and hangs on every phrase, basking in his message of love.

A letter like this awaits you. Composed with anticipation, hope, and love. It's a love letter from your Beloved.

Parts of the Bible probably don't seem much like a love letter in content, but believe it—God went to great lengths to compose His thoughts and preserve them for millennia. He eagerly awaits the moment your eyes light up when you open the Bible and realize this is His gift to you, an expression of His love as He reveals Himself and His intentions.

God wants us to accept His love letter, to read and reread it, to rush to it with a racing heart. Do I shake with anticipation when I read His Word? Do I pore over every phrase with an attitude of expectancy? Do I bask in the personal, precious words intended just for me?

God is not limited by His recorded words. But He has gone to great lengths, from a human perspective, for us to have this message of love. He has used the faithfulness of scribes and translators, archaeologists and monks, printers and publishers to speak to us—His beloved.

So we listen for His voice. We slow down and listen. And through this glorious, rich, full, long love letter, the Holy Bible, we hear Him. We study His written Word not just to gain knowledge, but *to know God!* To know what makes His eyes light up and His heart beat fast. To know what He desires.

HEARING GOD'S WORDS

Does God sometimes seem silent—even when you're listening as closely as you can? He may *seem* mute on a particular issue, especially one you're feeling anxious about. But when we have access to Scripture, whether to a physical Bible or to memorized verses locked inside the diary of our hearts, God is never silent. He is continuously communicating His commitment to us, His justice and compassion, and our value and worth. He is always saying, "I love you," "I forgive you," "Cast your cares on Me."

God is always speaking because *He has already spoken.* Scripture doesn't preclude the other ways He speaks, but it is our primary means of hearing from God, and we measure all other potential messages against it.

Our Lord speaks creatively, unexpectedly, and often. Still, coming back to Scripture is the safest place to interpret and evaluate the other possible messages God may be trying to get across to us. The truth is here. Through the study of God's Word—however in-depth or abbreviated—we hear Him.

You'll find bookstores packed with books to help you study Scripture, so I'm not going to attempt an in-depth approach in these few pages. But I can give you a few ideas. For instance, you might try reading the Bible systematically. Have some kind of plan—perhaps to read through Psalms and Proverbs, or to read through the entire Bible in a year. You might want to study the same passages your pastor is teaching from. What the plan is matters less than the fact that you have one.

You could also leave Bibles in every room with a bookmark at your spot. Update the bookmarks on cleaning days or when you are working in that room. Then, even if you have time only for a pit-stop moment of study, you will have a greater chance of grasping the context of the passage.

Whenever you study Scripture, listen to Jesus. When He was baptized by John, a voice from heaven declared, "This is my Son, whom

I love. Listen to him!" (Mark 9:7). Go to Scripture specifically to hear from Jesus, the Son of God. Study His life. Study His words. Read the Gospels back to back, concentrating on the "red letters," those passages where Jesus' words are set apart in red ink in some Bibles. What did He say to His closest companions? What did He say to people in pain?

Listen through Jesus' example, too. How can we learn from what He chose to do and not to do? Where did He go when He needed time alone? How did He handle betrayal? Spend an entire summer in the Gospels, and see what He has to say to you through the life He lived on earth. Listen to Him!

"Divine Reading"

You may have found a way to carve out time alone with God in your life as a monthly, weekly, or even daily date. In-depth study of Scripture is a natural "fit" if you have regular chunks of solitude in your schedule. When done in a meditative, interactive way, Bible study can be an intimate addition to your time alone with God, helping you to listen well.

Let me tell you about a way of studying God's Word that has helped me to see it as a real love letter. In her book *A Tree Full of Angels,* Benedictine nun Macrina Wiederkehr describes her order's method of Bible study, *lectio divina* (Latin for "divine reading"). The method is similar to that described in Christian author Evelyn Christenson's book *Lord, Change Me.*

Christenson suggests that before we read a passage of Scripture we pray, "Lord, change me." Then, she says, we should read *expecting to be changed.* Wiederkehr's advice is similar: "Always read the Scriptures with a heart ready to repent." She describes *lectio divina* as a special and unique way to read Scripture, slowly and reflectively, "reading with a longing to be touched, healed, and transformed by the Word."

Wiederkehr continues, "To be fully nourished by the richness hidden in these words you must hover over them slowly and reverently as one who is certain of finding a treasure.... [S]earch calmly and with assurance. You will find the treasure. You will be fed. You will be transformed."[2]

Both Christenson and Wiederkehr suggest that God Himself will stop us at the point where our personal "treasure" lies. But they also make it clear we can't take the treasure out of context. We must work to understand the passage or phrase that stands out to us in the greater context of the chapter or book. Who was speaking? To whom was it addressed? Some basic information about the author and the historical context will protect us from making false assumptions about the meaning of a passage.

When God does stop us at some particular verse or thought and we've come to a basic understanding of it—what then? What do we do with it? Think for a moment of Mary, the mother of Jesus. Remember how she responded to the hubbub of angels and shepherds and the townspeople's response to the birth of Jesus? "Mary treasured up all these things and pondered them in her heart" (Luke 2:19).

The phrase is recorded about her again, after a "bad mom day" incident in Jerusalem when Mary and Joseph lost track of twelve-year-old Jesus. They searched everywhere and eventually found Him in the temple courts, sitting among the teachers. He was obedient, the Bible says, and returned to Nazareth with His parents. And again Mary listened, wondered, pondered, and "treasured all these things in her heart" (Luke 2:51).

Listening to God through Scripture isn't any more mystical or difficult than doing what Mary did when she observed, listened to, and followed Jesus. Like her, we watch, read, learn, take everything in, and treasure it all in our hearts. When we sense that God is stopping us at some personal treasure—and we understand it in context—we then turn it over in our minds. We listen, wonder, and ponder.

First we ask God why. *Why stop me here, Lord? What are You saying to me?* Ask Him to guide you, perhaps to bring to mind other verses from Scripture that relate. Is there a thread to follow? Live with the passage for a while. Repeat it on the way to the office. Check your journal to see if something in this passage is an answer to your requests or concerns.

When we meditate on a passage of Scripture in this way, we extend an invitation to Christ Jesus to let it penetrate the innermost places of our hearts. His Word is called the sword of the Spirit. Having a sharp sword poking around inside can be painful. Dangerous. The Word of God is living and active, judging the thoughts and attitudes of the heart. Meditating on it—pondering the treasures God reveals—requires that we bare our souls before Him. It is an intimate act. Invasive even. It opens us up to God so He can change us.

I like the synonym a friend uses for meditation: "I'll *ruminate* on that awhile," she says. I wonder if she knows that "ruminate" also means "to chew the cud." I grew up on a farm where my dad raised Black Angus cattle; I spent lazy days tossing rocks into the pond as the cows stood nearby chewing the cud. As you probably know, after a cow swallows its meal, the grain is returned to its mouth for additional chewing, which makes for a most thorough digestive process. My father's Black Angus seemed never to stop chewing.

When you go through the day meditating on a passage of Scripture—"ruminating"—you repeat it over and over, you think about it, and then you think about it some more. Perhaps you think you've got it figured out. Then you bring it up again and think about it some more. Meditation is digesting spiritual truth as thoroughly as a cow chews its cud.

If you haven't lost your appetite, I encourage you to experiment with this process: Meditation. Rumination. Chewing the cud. Call it what you will, but take the time to ponder God's Word. The result will be rich nourishment to your soul.

CONTEMPLATIVE BIBLE READING

Richard Peace in his recent book *Contemplative Bible Reading: Experiencing God Through Scripture* outlines a similar "chewing the cud" approach to Bible study. He writes that in today's culture, there is a "growing desire to know the Bible in more than just a cognitive way." Not only understanding the Bible text, but hearing God's Word through the words we read make Bible reading "a form of prayer." Peace's wise and practical thoughts on *lectio divina* are worth repeating here:

The Process of Contemplative Bible Reading

"Contemplative Bible reading is both a simple and a profound way to approach Scripture. It consists of a four-part movement, beginning with the text and ending in prayer. This style of Bible reading can be used by both individuals and groups. The four steps that make up contemplative Bible reading are

"1. Reading/Listening: Read aloud a short passage of Scripture. As you read, listen for the word or phrase that speaks to you. What is the Spirit drawing your attention to?

"2. Meditating: Repeat aloud the word or phrase to which you are drawn. Make connections between it and your life. What is God saying to you by means of this word or phrase?

HOLDING HIM TO OUR HEARTS

The practice of listening to God through contemplative reading of the Bible—or through nature, or our children, or any of the other means by which He speaks to us—creates a richness in our relationship with Him that begs for even more. We want not only to hear

---

> "3. Praying: Now take these thoughts and offer them back to God in prayer, giving thanks, asking for guidance, asking for forgiveness, and resting in God's love. What is God leading you to pray?

> "4. Contemplating: Move from the activity of prayer to the stillness of contemplation. Simply rest in God's presence. Stay open to God. Listen to God. Remain in peace and silence before God. How is God revealing himself to you?"[3]

Peace goes on to address the valuable outcomes of *lectio divina*:

> "1. We learn to approach a passage in Scripture prayerfully, asking God to speak to us through it. We have new expectation when we come to the Bible. We know the power of reading the passage aloud and have learned to listen carefully.

> "2. We learn to mull over what we hear in such a way that we identify how it connects with our lives. Meditation becomes a reflex.

> "3. We learn to offer what we discover to God in prayer. Bible reading and prayer become one process.

> "4. We learn to stay open to God in the silence of prayer. We learn about deep resting in the presence of God but do not feel guilty if that does not happen. We know prayer is what God gives us."[4]

our Beloved's voice; we want to hold Him close to our hearts.

I can think of at least two ways to do just that: memorizing scripture; and creating memorials to remember and celebrate the specific ways God has spoken and continues to speak to each of us.

Memorizing Scripture

Memorizing scripture out of a sense of duty or because "that's what good Christians do" is rather uninspiring. When I realize that memorization is a way to preserve what my Beloved says to me, however, I am drawn to work at it. I have seen firsthand how God uses truths I've consciously made a part of my life as another way to reach me. Verses pop into my head at undeniably appropriate moments.

For example, I have clamped shut my mouth when I was about to speak or deleted huge passages from letters or e-mails when God dredged up in me the memorized verse "Even a fool is thought wise if he keeps silent, and discerning if he holds his tongue" (Proverbs 17:28). I memorized that long ago, when I had a significant problem with my tongue, but I'm embarrassed to admit that God, um, continues to use it in my life today.

During an especially difficult time in my life, the Lord used one memorized verse in particular to sustain me: "In this world you will have trouble. But take heart! I have overcome the world" (John 16:33). It was so comforting to hear God saying, in essence, "I know what you're going through, Ann, and it's only for a time. Hang in there. You're going to make it! I have overcome all of this, and I am going to get you through."

And these days, when I feel like saying something sharp to my children in response to a stressful situation, the verse, "[D]o not exasperate your children" (Ephesians 6:4) often comes to mind. It's addressed to

"Fathers," but it is for me just as well. I can exasperate them, frustrate them, and certainly can injure their spirits with harsh words. If I explode and say something anyway, I sit in a pool of regret. Then the Lord can bring to mind 1 John 1:9: "If we confess our sins, he is faithful and just and will forgive us our sins and purify us from all unrighteousness." God is so good. I confess and He forgives. And I can go back and apologize to the children and explain what I did that was wrong and ask for their forgiveness. They, too, are forgiving.

With God's words written indelibly on my heart, I'm not limited to listening to them only when I have a Bible in front of me. I can be anywhere and still hear my Lord's voice as He brings to mind whatever it is I happen to need: a loving phrase, a convicting command, something specific to share with a friend or stranger. My efforts at memorization result in His being able to draw from a reservoir of truth to reach me anytime, anywhere.

Having Scripture close to my heart helps me when I need to advise the children too: "Now, Sophie, you want Nathalie to be nice to you, don't you? Then you need to be nice to her too. 'Do to others what you would have them do to you'!" (Matthew 7:12).

We can give our kids the gift of a childhood filled with loving truths: how God feels about them, what He's done for them, what He has in store for them. Scripture verses engraved on our hearts are always there when we need them—and when our children need them. We have the opportunity to pack God's truth into *their* minds and hearts as well. Select verses to memorize *with* your children. As you and they increase the Word of God stored within, God is freer to communicate with you. Post verses on a mirror, quiz each other, learn sign language for key words, draw symbols to jog your memory. Do everything you can to hold God and His truths in your heart and the hearts of your children. You'll all have truths to ponder for a lifetime.

Creating Memorials

One spring several years ago our pastor asked people to bring in stones to symbolically represent how God had been faithful to them. After the congregation had brought up their stones and shared family and personal stories about how God had worked in their lives, we had an impressive pile near the front of the sanctuary.

Our pastor explained that the pile was to be our "Ebenezer," a memorial to God's work in the people of our church. (*Ebenezer* means "stone of help.") After the service we moved that huge pile of stones to a patch of grass outside the church. It was a curiosity to visitors who saw it on their way in. If they asked, we explained its significance to us.

This simple idea was modeled after the way the Israelites in the Old Testament often set up stones or piles of stones as altars or memorials to God. It got my family to thinking: Why not create a personal Ebenezer to represent God's help in our own lives? Besides, we love to collect stones. A friend suggested we create an Ebenezer jar and begin collecting stones that could be written on. We loved the idea. Now when God answers a prayer, we write it out, along with the date, either directly on one of the rocks or on a piece of paper that we tie around a rock. Then we place it in a see-through jar and watch the collection grow—a visual record of God's faithfulness to communicate with us as He acts on our prayers.

You could modify the idea by keeping an inside or outside rock garden, collecting stones as visual symbols of God's messages to you at various times in your life. Hannah Hurnard's book *Hind's Feet on High Places* provides great inspiration for gathering rocks to memorialize God's work in our lives.

However you do it, somehow record on a regular basis what God is saying to you through Scripture and other means and how you are responding to Him. Preserve your insights, God's reassurances, and convictions to act on. Use any system that works for your personality, from keeping an Ebenezer jar to jotting notes on three-by-five-inch cards to keeping an in-depth journal. For you nonjournalers, your record might be as simple as a one-sentence summary at the bottom of your daily planner.

As you preserve on an ongoing basis both what God is saying to you and what you are saying back to Him, you will have your own private, personal set of love letters—a precious reminder to hold your Beloved always close to your heart.

MOMS SPEAK OUT

Barb: Early on, I remember hearing God speak to me one time after I yelled at the girls and sent them to their room in a fit of anger. I knelt at my own bed, crying out to the Lord, feeling utterly defeated, knowing that I had overreacted and behaved so immaturely *again*. I had just begun to get a glimpse of what it meant to have a personal relationship with God and had heard that there actually were things in the Bible that could help me. I picked up my Bible, which had hardly ever been opened, and started leafing through the pages. My eyes fell on Psalm 32:8: "I will instruct you and teach you in the way which you should go; I will counsel you with My eye upon you" (NASB). Wow! I still remember how I felt as I realized that I was in partnership with the Lord when it came to being a mom and that somehow He would show me how to do this. I wrote in the margin "God's promise," not realizing He had thousands more. Now it sounds so elementary, but then it was a startling revelation—that God could actually come alongside me and help me to function.

Sharon: A very structured friend of mine divides her journal into sections marked "Praise and Thanksgiving," "Confession," and "Requests," or something like that. She records answered prayer and enjoys looking back on the things that God has done. Maybe I should use her method—if I saw "Confession" staring me in the face every day, then maybe I'd start confessing more!

Ruth: My one tool for solitude is to keep a pencil in hand and a piece of paper to write down the thoughts that I believe come back from God. It's not like real journaling but is just to capture the essence of what I seem to hear back. Frequently it's only a line or two. Even when I don't understand it at the time, I write it down and am often amazed at how much better I understand what God meant by it later on.

Beth: The Spirit can be unpredictable, and if He's like the wind, I guess my quiet times reflect that. Some days I know I pray because there are things that are really heavy on my heart. My prayers are sincere; I'm not just going through the motions; I'm there with the Lord. But I don't necessarily hear Him or feel connected. Other times I have experiences with Him that are unbelievable. This morning, reading in Proverbs, I felt as if God gave me verses for a situation that I had been crying out to Him about. Those vibrant times are frequent, but I also have times where I don't necessarily hear Him answer.

Lisa: My prayer is that Scripture becomes more than exciting stories for my kids. I pray that God will breathe life into them through the Bible. May they cling to God's Word as if it's a ring buoy afloat on a stormy sea.

Sharon: Changing terminology has helped me. I don't necessarily want to box God into thirty-minute segments—although that time is great! So instead of using the term "Quiet Time" and assigning thirty minutes for it, now I just say, "How's God going to speak with me?" It can be through time in the Word, or time with my kids, or listening to music, or while I'm out for a run.

Anita: I wish I hadn't let art and music and certain things that I love take a backseat in my life. For a long time I didn't do anything that wasn't sort of "Christian." I love art, many different forms of art, and art really speaks to me. I love to see the way colors work together, and I enjoy putting them together and making things look beautiful. It doesn't seem very "spiritual" that I love color, yet it totally draws me to God because it immediately makes me aware of His creativeness. He made color. He made us in such a way that we have the ability to enjoy color. It affects our environment, our moods. There's so much just in that one thing that helps me see Him in a broader way. I am starting to see in art the depth of God.

Susan G.: Over the last six months or year I've discovered something about myself. The more mature I become as a Christian, the more I seem to be able to decipher God's voice from other voices. His voice seems so much louder and clearer and distinguishable. The Bible says anything good is from the Lord, so I can assume that any good thought that pops into my head is from the Lord. When I've been struggling with a relationship and all of a sudden a voice pops into my head, "Forgive her, love her, go easy on her," I know those kind words are from God. Or maybe I'm having a really hard day with my kids: "Lord, give me wisdom. Help know how to handle this with the kids." It could be minutes, hours, or even days later, and a thought will pop into my head directly related to what I prayed. Because it is good and seems wise, I can trust that it is definitely from God. Maturity brings clarity.

Chapter 6

Taking His Advice

You are my friends if you do what I command.

JOHN 15:14

As moms, we know all about commands.

"Eat your peas."

"Stop poking that pencil in your brother's ear!"

"Write only on the paper, not on your great-grandmother's hand-stitched quilt!"

"Go to bed."

"Go *back* to bed."

"Time to get up. *Now.*"

Yep, we know a little something about authority, disobedience, and consequences. We understand the need for someone to act on our advice or respond quickly and without question to our direct requests and commands.

"Never run into the street."

"Don't talk to strangers."

"Just say no."

It doesn't take much study of either the Old or New Testament to discover that God has laced the Scriptures with His commands. Our Father and Creator, our trustworthy King, has commanded us to obey.

Of all people, we moms can appreciate the necessity of following through with His commands. Immediately.

The problems come when we try to carry out the commands. We know *that* from motherhood too. We see how children struggle to obey. Take a trip to the grocery store, and near some cart down almost any aisle you'll see it: children ignoring, smarting back, or disobeying in some way. But children aren't the only ones who choose sometimes to disobey. Uh-oh. God must be frustrated and disappointed with me too.

Something we may not fully appreciate, however, is this: When the Lord asks us to obey, there is an added dimension. Our relationship with Christ offers something no other relationship can—something we ourselves can't offer even to our own children.

Christ *empowers and enables us* to do the very thing that He asks. You've read John 15:5 before? "I am the vine; you are the branches. If a man remains in me and I in him, he will bear much fruit; apart from me you can do nothing."

Apart from Him, we can do nothing. Nothing. We can't obey. We can't do anything that will expand the kingdom of heaven. Even the really nice things we might do will have only temporal impact if done apart from Christ. Our attempts to obey through our own efforts may be noble and impressive, but they won't transform us—or anyone else.

THE POWER TO OBEY

When Christ tells us to obey, He doesn't point His finger and march us over to do it alone. By the mystery of the indwelling Spirit, Christ will actually do it through us. God does not command anything He isn't willing to move in us and do Himself. What may seem impossible, is possible with God—and *through* God.

If I try to exercise patience on my own, I may be able to employ a few deep-breathing techniques to keep calm for a moment. I can count to ten to delay an outburst. Those attempts at self-control are helpful, but they don't free Christ to transform me. Power is available to me—to you, too! The same power that raised Christ from the dead is mine at every moment. Why don't I access it?

We live in a self-help culture. Maybe we feel we *can* do it on our own? Tapes and seminars offer strategic plans for inner transformation. They suggest ways to cope with stress and deal with difficult people; they offer plans to attain our dreams and raise healthy kids. While some offer ridiculous ideas, others have innovative, useful suggestions. If we can manage to find the ones with legitimate, good ideas, why not use them?

We can. But they will only go so far. Why? Because of Christ—or rather, the lack of Christ. The ideas are just ideas if we are doing them apart from Christ. If Christ Himself isn't moving through us, "we can do nothing."

Obeying the Lord Jesus Christ—obeying His commands, following *His* truth, and drawing from His strength to do the very thing He is asking or commanding—allows Him to empower us in ways we only dream of happening any other way! The impact a seminar might have promised is miniscule compared to the eternal, supernatural impact possible through Christ Himself working in us and through us. *His* commands need *His* empowerment to be followed through as *He* desires.

When Christ commands us to do something, our part is an active yieldedness. In other words, we do have a part in responding to God. We need to say, "I will" to God, not "I will obey, on my own, *if it's the last thing I do*." We could try with grit and determination to follow through, but Christ is offering something better. He commands us to do something, and we say, "I will…by Your enabling, Lord." We need both elements. Active: "I will." Yielded: "I want and choose to, but I can't without Your supernatural enabling, Lord Jesus."

It's nice to hear admiration for something we do. "You are so patient with your kids. I wish I were more like you." "You seem to manage your outside job and mothering so well." Does our human desire to be recognized for our efforts and abilities hinder us from absolute obedience? Perhaps. And I think that's why sometimes Christ asks—commands—us to do ignoble acts of service as part of humbling us to depend on Him.

Some writers on the spiritual disciplines recommend self-imposed acts of secrecy in order to develop humility. The element of secrecy eliminates pride, they say—no one can brag on you.

Clearly, these writers are not moms. How many more secret acts would we need to build into our lives beyond what we already have? Motherhood offers countless opportunities for secretive service. In fact, that seems like a great summary of what motherhood is all about: secretly, quietly, humbly serving a household of people with little or no recognition or thanks. No one brags on us. Frankly, I think we've got that discipline pretty much covered every time we fold and put away the laundry, stay up all night with a feverish child, clean mud off the carpet that the neighbor kids tracked in, serve snacks to those same kids, pack a lunchbox with a son's favorite food, or leave work early to attend a daughter's track meet.

Each time we fill some aspect of our mom role, we are likely offering the Lord multiple acts of secretive service to others. When we think of those acts as opportunities to eliminate pride and focus on the Lord, it can minimize our feelings of martyrdom and maximize our sense of servanthood. Think of it—a built-in discipline! An opportunity to grow more humble and Christlike that we needn't go out of our way to create. Motherhood is a gift! Quit laughing—I'm serious! I'll admit that when I'm secretly cleaning up the dried cheese cubes my daughter must have absent-mindedly placed in the bottom cabinet a week ago, I don't always think of it as an act of service. But it certainly would be freeing if I did.

If your built-in acts of service aren't enough and pride is still a problem, additional acts of secrecy may be necessary. Well, we're creative women. We can easily come up with ideas. No one needs to know how many hours you spend on the phone counseling your best friend during a crisis or how much cash you slipped into the coat pocket of a friend who's struggling. Weed your neighbor's garden while she's at work. Send flowers to a friend who is in the midst of a divorce. Some of our secretive acts of service can be out of the household and into the world. Just think of some needs, and go meet them without telling anyone. Simple as that.

In my own life Christ has called me to enough specific, secret acts of obedience for my family and beyond that I haven't needed to invent many extras. He has prompted me to actions more surprising and secretive than I ever would have invented on my own. The fact that some of these calls to obedience are even a bit strange challenges my spiritual commitment in a healthy way: Am I willing to yield to God's leadership even when it stretches me? Am I willing to accept His empowerment to follow through on His command no matter what He asks?

I don't think I will compromise my intimacy with the Lord if I tell you about one request He made of me years ago. I was working full-time at a church that prepared Sunday morning services as outreach events. The planning team and everyone involved always felt burdened to pray for the people who might come each week. So that was always in my heart.

But one Sunday morning I awoke very early—that in itself seemed like pretty clear communication from God! It's highly unusual for me to awaken on my own, let alone to awaken *early!* I felt burdened with an urgent thought—a thought so specific that I can't imagine I would have come up with it on my own: I clearly sensed that God was telling me to go down to the church and walk through the entire parking lot, stepping in and praying for each and every parking spot…or rather, praying for the people in the cars that might potentially fill each spot.

I don't remember exactly what my initial reaction was, except I'm sure I resisted. The whole idea seemed a little silly and unnecessary. At the same time, it seemed as if God was pressing me to do it as an act of obedience. The longer I lay on my bed trying to talk myself out of it, the more my gut churned.

The urgency remained, so I yielded. Actively. I said something like, "Okay, Lord. I don't really want to do this, but I will. This is Your thing, but You want me in on it. So…if You move through me, I'll do it."

So I did. I weaved through that parking lot, stepping in each space, praying for each person in each car. It reminded me of the "battle" of Jericho: Each day for a week Joshua led Israel to march one time around the city, silently, with only the sound of trumpets leading the parade. On the seventh day they marched around it seven times, the priests blew the trumpets, the people shouted and—splat! The walls came a-tumblin' down. The Israelites followed through with God's bizarre marching orders, and God did the rest.

It sounds strange, but that was God's plan for Joshua. It makes God's request for me to walk around a parking lot seem pretty tame. It's comforting, though, to realize that God has called His people, leaders, and prophets to some bizarre things.

To this day I can only guess why the Lord asked me to do that. No one has ever told me a story of God transforming him or her that I can trace back to that morning. But I listened and obeyed, and by God's enabling, something secretly transpired in the kingdom. Perhaps some spiritual walls came tumbling down as someone stepped out of his car that day. I just needed to be willing to hear and respond to the Lord's request so that He could walk with me through that parking lot. *With* me—and *through* me.

Sometimes that's how our acts of obedience are. God asks something of us that we do through His enabling, yet He may never reveal why He asked us to do it in the first place.

FOLLOWING FIRST IMPRESSIONS

My urgent wake-up call that morning falls into a category I refer to as "impressions." There's this sensation—often almost physical—that God is pressing against me and insisting I follow through with something. Sometimes He wants me to make a phone call or have a conversation with a neighbor, and I can't shake the pressure to follow through. Sometimes He asks me to perform an act of service or secretly give something to someone. A friend of mine has an amusing description for this kind of "impression." She says, "I feel as if God is pressing His big thumb down on top of my head, smashing down on me until I follow through with whatever He asks."

Is the concept of getting "impressions" from God a new one? Are you afraid you won't be able to tell a God-given impression from an idea of your own? Ideas are constantly rattling around in our heads to do something or call someone. Something as simple as baking cookies for a neighbor could be a great idea of your own or loaded with eternal possibilities if God is behind it. If you are gifted with discernment, you may naturally know whether your idea is from you or from God. In some instances, it won't matter. Taking cookies to a neighbor is certainly an act of kindness you can't go wrong with. Other times, you might have a bizarre thought (like my parking-lot walk), and you'd only do it if you knew it was from Him.

To figure out whether or not your impressions are God-given, practice paying attention to them when they come. Don't just let them flit into your mind and out again. Write them down. Ask, "Lord, is this from You?" or "Which one of these is from You?" Talk to God enough to decide whether or not to carry it out. Does it agree with what Scripture teaches? Is it aligned with Truth? Rule out any idea that would lead to sin. If you think the idea is (or may be) from God and is in agreement with Scripture, follow through with it, by His enabling. Follow up afterward to see if there is any indication or affirmation that it was indeed God's idea and not your own. You may realize later it was just a nice idea of your own. That's fine. But over-all, err on the side of obedience. We can find great value in listening to these "impressions" of God.

Following Personal Convictions

A more frequent way God commands us to do something is by con-victing us through Scripture. When Scripture leaps out at me, I explore the idea that God might want me to pay closer attention.

Flipping through the Bible I used through college and into early adulthood, I see evidence of these personal convictions and how God changed me. One thing I recall and see clues of (by my markings) is that God was stopping me on every verse that had to do with the tongue. "Even a fool, when he keeps silent, is considered wise; When he closes his lips, he is counted prudent" (Proverbs 17:28, NASB). "[L]et everyone be quick to hear, slow to speak and slow to anger" (James 1:19, NASB). "And the tongue is a fire, the very world of iniquity" (James 3:6, NASB). Verses like these are circled, underlined, and highlighted or found their way into frequent confessions in my journals, as I felt God clearly com-manding me to stop dominating conversations.

Whether or not I was actually sinning, there was still a healthy principle at work: "When words are many, sin is not absent, but he who holds his tongue is wise" (Proverbs 10:19). The Lord Jesus Christ wanted to transform me, so He made a request. Offered some advice. Issued a command. "Shhhh. Let someone else have a chance to talk, Ann. Listen. Listen to Me and to others."

Patterns of sin are nearly impossible to break without the transforming power of Christ. When He commands, He gives us the power we need to obey. Except for the scriptural conviction, I can't quite explain how God actually transformed my tendency to dominate conversations, but there came a time when I realized I was talking less and listening more. Even though I may have made some efforts of my own, I believe the imperceptible changes came about through Christ. It took years. Years and years. And anyone who knows me can assure you that I am still not lacking for words. As I mentioned earlier, God still has to bring Proverbs 17:28 to my mind occasionally. But not as often as before. And by God's grace, He has helped me learn to listen better. Transformation through the love of Christ, not grit and determination, has changed my relationships and friendships profoundly.

The rich relationship with the Lord we've been discussing at length in this book is a prerequisite to obedience. Knowing the Lord Jesus Christ, being known by Him, is all part of it. When we trust Him enough to pour out our hearts to Him, He is freed up to work in us. When we are in step with the Spirit, walking with Him, the commands don't come out of the blue. They come out of our intimacy with Christ. They come out of study and listening. The other chapters in this book illustrate some of the principles that lead us to intimacy. And only then, as we know and lean on the leadership of our Lord, can we obey the way He wants us to, in that state of active yieldedness.

In fact, if you aren't seeing change in your life, if you don't see transformation, if you feel like screaming, "This isn't working!"—don't get frustrated. Don't try harder. Don't *do* more. Go back to the earlier chapters of this book, and focus on your relationship with the Lord. Know Him. Transformation is so dependent on your relationship with God, it is essential that you go back and concentrate on getting to know the Savior.

A Time to Reflect

Besides the specific things God might ask us to do—such as walk and pray through a parking lot or be quick to hear and slow to speak—what are other commands we're expected to obey through Christ? Scan Scripture, and God's commandments pop out as clearly as those we bark at our own children. But the one that rises above the rest by overwhelming repetition is *love*.

"Love the Lord your God with all your heart and with all your soul and with all your mind." This is the first and greatest commandment. And the second is like it: "Love your neighbor as yourself." (Matthew 22:37-39)

Love your enemies and pray for those who persecute you, that you may be sons of your Father in heaven. (Matthew 5:44-45)

A new command I give you: Love one another. As I have loved you, so you must love one another. (John 13:34)

My command is this: Love each other as I have loved you. Greater love has no one than this, that he lay down his life for his friends. You are my friends if you do what I command.... This is my command: Love each other. (John 15:12-14,17)

Dear friends, if our hearts do not condemn us, we have confidence before God and receive from him anything we ask, because we obey his commands and do what pleases him. And this is his command: to believe in the name of his Son, Jesus Christ, and to love one another as he commanded us. Those who obey his commands live in him, and he in them. (1 John 3:21-24)

And he has given us this command: Whoever loves God
must also love his brother. (1 John 4:21)

And this is love: that we walk in obedience to his commands.
As you have heard from the beginning, his command is that
you walk in love. (2 John 6)

I think God wants to be sure we "get it." There's a bunch of other
stuff He wants us to do too—and stuff He *doesn't* want us to do. But
our Savior is asking us—commanding us—to love. Love Him. Love
one another. Even love our enemies.

Here's a list of other commands I found in a quick scan of Scripture. See if you can add to it. Thoughtfully read over the list, and if
something stands out, ask God why.

- Pray without ceasing.
- Rejoice in the Lord always.
- Go make disciples of all nations.
- If your right hand causes you to sin, cut it off and throw it away.
- Give to the one who asks you…do not turn away from the one
  who wants to borrow from you.
- Do not store up for yourselves treasures on earth.
- Do not worry about tomorrow.
- Do not judge.
- Ask. Seek. Knock.
- Wash one another's feet.
- Repent, and be baptized.
- Obey your parents; honor your father and mother.
- Do not exasperate your children.
- Submit to one another.
- Do everything without complaining.

The Lord Jesus Christ has every right to tell us what to do, what to
stop doing, and what to do on His behalf. We don't need to know why

though He often lets us know anyway. All we need to do is act on it. To do it. To obey without relying on our own puny efforts. That's the amazing thing, the miracle: The same God who commands us to love *is* love and loves through us. Through our yielded hearts.

How else can we love our enemies and pray for those who persecute us, except that Christ does it through us? We might manage to mouth a prayer or go through some motions of love. But life-transforming love that finds its way through the pain of relationships and comes out still loving even when hated and giving even when never receiving—that kind of love flows through us only from Christ Himself.

When people look at our families, they should see peace, love, kindness, gentleness, self-control—not the fruits of spectacular human effort from moms devoted to creating this mood or environment, but the fruits of a spectacular God who gave His Spirit to us to do these things in us.

We need to respond to Him by being willing to obey. Our effort is to step out in faith—not faith that *we* can love, but faith that Christ will pull off the very thing that He asks.

MOMS SPEAK OUT

Ruth: One time I felt a strong urge to call a friend I hadn't talked to in a couple of years, but I didn't do it. I just kept talking myself out of it. She called me a few weeks later, and it turned out during that same time her son was trying to commit suicide. I told her, "God did not fail you. *I* failed you. *He* did everything He needed to do to get me to call you, and I didn't do it."

Linda Z.: Every day I pray that I will have an ear to hear. Every day I pray that I will have the courage to do whatever He would have me do.

It takes a committed effort to say deliberately every day, "I want to do this." I don't want to let a day go by where I don't experience Him.

Susan G.: The Bible talks about those who have ears to hear and eyes to see. I think that's developed in my heart over time. I've learned how to listen to God, and I recognize His voice more clearly than I used to when I was younger. I can now distinguish it from the voice of the flesh, what my own desires are. The deeper my relationship goes with God, the more I can "taste" what He's like. The more I taste what He's like, the less I want to disappoint Him. When I hear His voice and He's asking me to do something, I want to respond to Him. If I don't respond, I would disappoint Him, and I don't want that.

Debbie: Can your little children look you square in the eye when they've disobeyed? In the same way, even little infractions keep us from looking God square in the eye. The more they build up—the longer we let them go—the harder it is to crawl up in His lap. He certainly wants us there—*we* are the ones with the problem!

Lisa: I cried yesterday when I punished my daughter after warning her several times to avoid the Christmas presents. I can't even imagine how much God wants to cry when I fail to obey His commands and promptings on matters of eternal significance—matters far more important than the problem of prematurely unwrapped gifts.

Susan M.: Obeying God makes me more dependent, not that I like being there, because I would most definitely rather be self-sufficient. But it keeps me on my knees, figuratively and sometimes literally.

Beth: Obedience is a whole lot different when it's grounded in relationship with Jesus Christ. It comes out of sheer gratitude and amazement for what He has been willing to do on my behalf. We tend to forget this with our kids because we want to be sure that they get the rules right. Not that we shouldn't teach the rules, but legalism comes out of fear. We need to help kids move their hearts toward God so God can get hold of their hearts and make a change. Jesus wants their hearts first. His having their hearts first is ultimately more important than the choices they make because they can't make the right choices unless He has their hearts. Ultimately it comes down to a relationship with Jesus.

Susan C.: I think I understand obedience to God better now that I'm a mother. If I ask my kids to obey, it's not to be cruel. There's love behind it. It's like that verse that says if your child asks for bread would you give him a stone. God doesn't give senseless commands. He loves us, and His love for us goes way beyond our love for our own children. You don't ask your kids to go pick up that toy because you want to make them sweat or want to teach them something. That seems like a silly comparison because God is so much above us and loves us so much more than we love our own children, but that's the context I can put it in because that's where I live. Whereas before I might have thought of it as more dictatorial, now I see commands are motivated by God's love. I think, too, as time has gone by, it's becoming clearer to me what God is asking; I'm getting the picture more. It doesn't mean I jump up and do the difficult things He asks, but I do see that He has a plan and that all these things He asks me to do are part of the plan. It goes back to His love.

Susan M.: Our kids being in the public school system has been an obedience thing for me. Finally this summer other doors started to close, and I started to "get it." God's been saying, "Susan, I'm putting you here. I'd like you to trust Me and watch Me work. Trust Me with your kids. You don't know the answers, but trust Me with them." Once I reached that point of being willing to be obedient, my total outlook changed.

Debbie: I'm really learning to trust Him! This teenager stuff is *hard.* It truly tests everything—our trust in Him primarily. But also trusting that He was there with us in the early, formative years and that His foundational truths we imparted then will help them through these challenging years. When I worry if I "did it right," He reminds me that He was there, that I was doing my best to hear Him and obey Him. It's just really scary!

Susan C.: God has asked me to move into people's lives: "You have to go see so-and-so. You need to call her, and you need to call her now." I think when I do things like that I realize it's God pushing me beyond my own limits. He gives us commands sometimes that force us out of our own lives and into other people's lives. Entering into someone's life is a really big issue of obedience I think because we live such self-centered lives.

Exploring the Great Outdoors

The heavens declare the glory of God; the skies proclaim the work of his hands.
Day after day they pour forth speech; night after night they display knowledge.

PSALM 19:1-2

In our synthetic, walled-in, air-conditioned existence, where can we find the things of creation? We enter our office complexes, hunker down in cubicles lit by fluorescent lights, buy lunch two floors down in the cafeteria, take our kids to indoor playgrounds. For safety or convenience reasons, we even exercise indoors. When do we lift up our eyes to the hills if all we're doing is lifting our eyes to Web sites and stoplights? When can we consider the lilies of the field if all we do is breeze past them on the interstate?

If our only exposure to the outdoors and nature occurs during a brisk, thirty-second walk across the asphalt parking lot of Target to our cars, something is missing. Growth in our relationship with our Creator will be stunted, as we will miss out on observing, valuing, and attempting to understand what is precious to Him.

When will we celebrate God's creativity and hear what He wants to say through His creation? What will it take to realize we are entirely dependent upon Him and His natural world to survive? "For by him all things were created: things in heaven and on earth, visible and invisible, whether thrones or powers or rulers or authorities; all things were created by him and for him. He is before all things, and in him all things hold together" (Colossians 1:16-17).

The false sense of security provided by supermarkets and convenience stores sometimes keeps me from fully appreciating that I am sustained by Jesus' powerful word, and that in Him all things hold together. Whether or not we realize it, we are just as dependent upon God's control of the natural world as people in Third World countries who may starve if a flood destroys their one field of crops.

Caroline Falconi, my sister-in-law, works as a program evaluator for organizations such as World Vision. She travels the world to discuss with the poor the challenges and problems they face. Several years ago as we were talking about the people she has met, I asked her about the Christians she's met among the poor. Caroline told me that she had noticed that the people who seemed to have the most intimate relationships with the Lord were those most intimate with the earth. "Each seed represents a possible future, so there's this look on their faces when they plant and look at the rain." She paused with a smile, seeming to recall that "look," then continued, "They're hopeful. They are utterly dependent upon the Lord for survival. If it doesn't rain, their crops die. In many ways they have a much deeper faith than most North American Christians I've known."

As one of those "North American Christians," this stuck with me. Caroline wasn't challenging me or trying to make me feel bad. She was responding to some of my questions in complete honesty, and I thank her for making me think.

Her comment made me look hard at my life. Was I so protected from the elements that I was lacking something in my faith in Christ? Was I anywhere near as intimate with Christ as the poor whom Caroline knew so well? Would getting in tune with the natural world help me know Him better? Did I need to dig in the dirt?

Just because most of us don't have to till soil, plant wheat, and wait several months before reaping, threshing, grinding, and finally using the grain to make a loaf of bread, doesn't mean we aren't dependent upon the Lord for its availability. But because I don't personally appreciate the precarious weeks of no rain, the tedium of waiting, and the concern that if this crop doesn't make it there won't be any bread at all, I wonder if I am as passionately grateful for my daily bread as I should be. Instead, like most of us, I just pick up a loaf at the 7-Eleven when I pay for my gas, M&Ms, and a newspaper. If I'm missing something because I too often forget that my daily bread comes literally from God's hand, I want to find it. For myself and for my children.

THE LESSONS OF NATURE

How do I live with growing appreciation and gratitude for Christ's sustenance through the natural world? How do I experience God through intimate knowledge of His creation?

In his book *The Lessons of St. Francis*, John Michael Talbot explores the life of Saint Francis, who reveled in nature and had an affinity with creation, to see if anything could apply to our lives today. Talbot suggests that a "simple way to practice reverence for creation is to grow a garden. There's nothing like getting your hands in the dirt to put you in touch with nature.... [E]ven if you live in a New York City high-rise you can start a window box. And everyone can learn to grow houseplants. Whether you grow flowers or tomatoes, the process is all a part of knowing more about the wonderful world we inhabit." Talbot goes on to urge the reader:

Seize the opportunity to walk in a park or drive through a forest with the windows down. As you're there in the midst of God's green earth, practice mindfulness, which is a way of meditating on what you see and the Creator who makes it

possible. Breathe in the aromas that surround you. Quiet
your heart and be aware that every step you take is on holy
ground. Tune into the symphony of the birds and the rustle
of the wind through the leaves. Thank God for the beauty of
creation, which includes you![1]

Simple ideas like these could seem a tad trite if it weren't for our
tendency to stay inside with the television on. I suggest we take some
guidance from Talbot and Saint Francis and nurture some plants, tune
in to the rustle of leaves and the beauty of creation. We have to start
somewhere, so watch the sunset tonight as the sky streaks rose and
orange. Gaze at the moon. Listen for the first true night sound. As Talbot quotes from William of Saint Thierry, "A man who has lost his
sense of wonder is a man dead."[2]

Tomorrow morning step outside and look to the upper branches
of the silver maple tree growing in your backyard or across the street
and read Sergeant Joyce Kilmer's poem:

TREES

I think that I shall never see
A poem lovely as a tree.

A tree whose hungry mouth is prest
Against the earth's sweet flowing breast;

A tree that looks at God all day
And lifts her leafy arms to pray;

A tree that may in Summer wear
A nest of robins in her hair;

Upon whose bosom snow has lain;
Who intimately lives with rain.

Poems are made by fools like me,
But only God can make a tree.[3]

Long before Sergeant Kilmer, another poet noted the power of observing God's creation:

Let the heavens rejoice, let the earth be glad;
    let the sea resound, and all that is in it;
    let the fields be jubilant, and everything in them.
Then *all the trees of the forest will sing for joy;*
    they will sing before the LORD, for he comes,
    he comes to judge the earth. (Psalm 96:11-13, emphasis mine)

A Primer on God's Character

Before we can join the rest of creation in singing praises to our God, we've got to get out into it! It shouldn't be that unnatural. The human race was designed to live in a perfect garden with no other shelter than what God provided in the natural world. God allowed Adam and Eve to tend the garden and draw nourishment and enjoyment from it. Something in us today should be able to relate to that. In fact, how would mankind and nature relate today had sin not entered the picture? We get a glimpse of how life might have been in Isaiah's prophecy of Christ's kingdom still to come—a kingdom restored to God's original vision, where the wolf will lie down with the lamb, the leopard with the kid, and the young lion with the calf, all in harmony (cf. Isaiah 11, NASB).

For the time being there may not be perfect harmony in nature, but there is still beauty, power—and a message. "[W]hat may be known about God is plain to them, because God has made it plain to them. For since the creation of the world God's invisible qualities—his eternal power and divine nature—have been clearly seen, being understood from what has been made, so that men are without excuse"

(Romans 1:19-20). A person who has never heard of God can't excuse herself, feigning ignorance, because God reveals His eternal power and divinity through creation.

Well, if God is revealing Himself to us through creation, we should listen! We should spend time with His creation and pay more careful attention. Observe. Make notes. Draw your own conclusions. Write your own psalm of praise based on what you observe as you sit before a stream, marveling at the minnows or laughing at the water bugs skimming across the surface of the water. What connections might be made to the story of Christ walking on water? What of God's creativity could be appreciated? What does He have to say to you? You will only find out when you step outside and go for a walk. Sit quietly. Watch. Sketch, perhaps. Wonder.

Read these excerpts from Psalm 104, in which the psalmist sees nature as an opportunity to explode in both metaphorical and literal response to all that he imagined or observed. I've included a long chunk so you can see more of the writer's process. He is inconsistent with his point of view, shifting from third person to first, talking about God and then naturally slipping into prayer. I find myself doing the same thing in my journals when something of God's creation takes my breath away.

Praise the LORD, O my soul.

O LORD my God, you are very great;
        you are clothed with splendor and majesty.
He wraps himself in light as with a garment;
        he stretches out the heavens like a tent
        and lays the beams of his upper chambers on their waters.
He makes the clouds his chariot
        and rides on the wings of the wind.
He makes winds his messengers,
        flames of fire his servants.

He set the earth on its foundations;
> it can never be moved.

You covered it with the deep as with a garment;
> the waters stood above the mountains.

But at your rebuke the waters fled,
> at the sound of your thunder they took to flight;

they flowed over the mountains,
> they went down into the valleys,
> to the place you assigned for them.

You set a boundary they cannot cross;
> never again will they cover the earth....

How many are your works, O LORD!
> In wisdom you made them all;
> the earth is full of your creatures....

These all look to you
> to give them their food at the proper time.

When you give it to them,
> they gather it up;

when you open your hand,
> they are satisfied with good things.

When you hide your face,
> they are terrified;

when you take away their breath,
> they die and return to the dust.

When you send your Spirit,
> they are created,
> and you renew the face of the earth.

I suggest you take those excerpts—better yet, look up and read all of Psalm 104—and let them inspire your own adaptation. Try processing that passage while on a hike, feeding a squirrel at a park, or simply watching the birds pecking away at your backyard bird-feeder (see verses 27-30). See if being in similar settings intensifies the energy of the poetry.

When my friend Sonya Waters and her husband, John, read that entire psalm at the top of Yosemite Falls in Yosemite National Park, she was struck with the way it made her look at nature as literally obeying God and fitting into His commands. Like Sonya, get out into God's creation to read that psalm, then look around you at the diversity of the natural world. Be amazed. If you feel so inspired, write a psalm of your own, a prayer with praise for who God is and what He is saying to you through His creation.

A Footnote to God's Word

Another benefit of understanding and appreciating God's creation is the light it casts on Scripture. After all, the psalmists weren't scratching away at their manuscripts on the top floor of a seminary library. They were outside, listening, smelling, and observing the world around them. Getting out in that world ourselves can illuminate their words in ways nothing else can.

The Bible was recorded in a predominantly agrarian world. There were cities, but people walked. There were businessmen, but they weren't confined to air-conditioned offices. Thus we constantly read references to nature as metaphors, such as when we will "soar on wings like eagles." Jesus, especially, built parables around the way His natural world works. He compared faith and His kingdom to a mustard seed and described the necessity of His death by reminding His disciples that a kernel of wheat must fall to the ground and die before it produces many seeds.

To appreciate how intimately the listeners or readers would have grasped these earthy comparisons, we must understand Christ's parables in their historical context. But we don't necessarily dismiss them and then come up with techno-inspired parables of our own. Just because the Bible was composed in cultures void of technology doesn't mean we have to update them by inventing "modern" or "post-modern" parables. Trees still grow. We still eat from the fruits of the fields. We are still dependent upon the natural world for our physical sustenance. That hasn't changed in two-thousand-plus years. I think God has a lot He wants to teach us through nature, and we are letting technology steal these messages.

As I understand the truth of how the Lord's world works—planting seeds myself, let's say, and understanding the "death" that produces growth—I am able to understand His parables without trying so hard. That's why Jesus told parables. They brought clarity to confusing, deep truths. They should bring clarity to us, too. It will only help us to familiarize ourselves more with the natural world.

The Gifts of Nature

Mary Pipher, Ph.D., author of *The Shelter of Each Other: Rebuilding Our Families*, describes several case studies of families in turmoil. She contrasts a family from the 1930s—her grandparents actually—with those families she sees currently in her counseling practice. Noting the strengths and weaknesses of each era, she draws some practical conclusions and offers suggestions that she has seen bring healing. After describing a family that struggled with typical suburban problems, Pipher writes:

> As adults, people remember three kinds of family events with great pleasure—meals, vacations and time outdoors. I wanted this family to have some memories.

"I'm going to make a couple of radical suggestions here," I said. "One is that you turn off the television and computer for at least a couple nights a week, and two, that the family do something out of doors every week. Watch a sunset, go for a walk or take a trip to a wilderness area."

These were standard suggestions for me. I think that the natural world has great power to heal and restore broken families. Children need contact with the natural world. It's an antidote to advertising and gives them a different perspective on the universe. Looking at the Milky Way makes most of us feel small and yet a part of something vast. Television, with its emphasis on meeting every need, makes people feel self-important and yet unconnected to anything greater than themselves.[4]

Just as Pipher suggested, turning off technology and getting out in nature has brought our family closer, and already we are seeing that those three kinds of family events remembered with pleasure are reality for us: meals, vacations, and time outdoors.

Camping includes all three! We have become avid campers, starting when Isabelle, our first daughter, was only sixteen months old. We anticipate these events, even if our trip is merely an hour's drive to a state park. Depending on where we go, we hike, splash in lakes or oceans, collect rocks or shells, and shiver or sweat inside our tent. The children recall these trips in great detail, and they often talk about their love for eating outside.

While it doesn't happen like clockwork, we do try to get outside a little bit every day and go on a "nature hike" once a week—with the exception of frigid winter days and the really gray, dreary, rainy days, too, I admit. I could take them out in rain slickers and galoshes, but I'm still kind of wimpy.

I also go through various phases of self-education about the natural world, and I've witnessed how my personal enthusiasm for stargazing, bird watching, or flower or tree identification is all I've needed to sustain the interest of my kids.

Even if I didn't read up on deciduous trees, though, kids love raking their leaves into piles and jumping into them. They love digging for worms. They love watering plants and watching things grow. How much better will they (and we) understand the parable of the sower if they have personally plucked rocks and fieldstones from a freshly tilled garden plot!

I have really appreciated Pipher's book. Her advice has already made a great impact on our family life. But I guess I'm greedy. I want more for my family than the unity created by our encounters with the natural world. I want my children to appreciate God's creation so that they will appreciate God Himself even more. I can't force that. I can merely let my own soul be touched by the Lord through contact with His fearsome, beautiful, amazing creation and then at appropriate moments reveal to the children what I have gained.

I have to admit I haven't always been such a nature lover. I used to be content to stay inside and let the girls create Lego and Lincoln Log masterpieces in the mud-free, indoor habitat of home. But in addition to Pipher's advice, the writings of Charlotte Mason are largely responsible for getting me off the couch and into the backyard. Her ideas, formed after a lifetime of constant involvement with educating British children in the 1800s, have inspired me to bundle up the kids and begin my own adventure of experiencing God in His creation.

Mason encouraged parents and educators alike to find the physical, educational, and most importantly the *spiritual* benefits of spending long hours outside with children. They—and I—found great success by applying her suggestions. My children and I have been transformed by appreciation for God's creativity as we've examined bark, moss, and mold; admired snowy tree crickets; and picked apart hickory nuts. And we're surely healthier for breathing in all that fresh air and chasing dragonflies at Cool Creek Park.

In one of her books, *Home Education*, Mason suggests the mother simply sit and read while the child makes his own observations. However, to encourage a spiritual moment, she suggests that "very rarely, and with tender filial reverence…for to touch on this ground with *hard* words is to wound the soul of the child," a mother might

> …point to some lovely flower or gracious tree, not only as a
> beautiful work, but a beautiful *thought* of God, in which we
> may believe He finds continual pleasure, and which He is
> pleased to see his human children rejoice in. Such a seed of
> sympathy with the Divine thought sown in the heart of the
> child is worth many of the sermons the man may listen to
> hereafter, much of the 'divinity' he may read.[5]

Ah, to reveal my own heart, touched by some exquisite beauty fashioned by my loving Creator—a *thought* of God in which He finds pleasure—that is an extraordinary gift to give my children! Rejoicing in the beauty of creation is a far cry from staring at the television. I pray that I am passing on a heritage of truth and wonder, as Isabelle, Sophie, and Nathalie see glimpses of God and hear from Him through the beauty of creation.

EXPERIENCING NATURE

We don't need to be an environmentalist or naturalist to increase our appreciation of God's creation. We don't need a cabin in the woods or a cottage by the seashore. Even if all we do is periodically step outside and stare at the sky—even a tiny patch of sky—we will begin to appreciate that which God alone created. Try some of these ideas:

Tips for the Reluctant Naturalist

- Instead of watching a talk show tomorrow afternoon, load up the kids in a wagon, pack a snack, and take a walk!

- Keep a nature journal. Try sketching and adding watercolors later. Look up the names of everything you study, and write them out. Adam was given the task of naming the animals. Recognizing and remembering the names given to the things of creation can help us appreciate their intrinsic value.

- Go camping. Easy for me to say? Okay, so I love camping. I'll admit it. I love torn jeans and hair up in a ponytail, no makeup, hiking, going to sleep surrounded by night sounds with nothing but thin nylon separating me from God's creation. Who knows? God may use camping in your life also to help you feel more connected and dependent on Him.

- Small children love nature. Learn to love it from them. Dig in the mud. Watch an anthill. Hold a snail in your hand. Lie on a blanket and watch clouds float past. See how children may inspire you to notice more.

- Go for a twenty-minute walk every day. Notice seasonal changes. Watch flowers bloom, flourish, fade, and develop seeds. Pay more attention as you go. It'll do wonders for your figure, your health, and your appreciation of the Creator.

- Read books by nature lovers like Annie Dillard, James Herriot, and Gerald Durrell. Their personal passion may turn you on to animals and living things in ways you never thought possible! And because your ultimate goal is to listen to God through them, you'll have an added dimension to your own journeys into the natural world.

- Read Job 39, then visit a zoo to appreciate the wide range of animals God created. Wonder at His creativity. What can you learn from the wallaby, emu, or lemur?
- Consider gardening at some level. If you've never gardened before, you can read books and talk with friends for ideas, but until you're digging in the soil yourself, you'll lack that first-hand knowledge of what God wants to say about Himself and about you.
- Pick a nature hobby. Bird watching, gardening, shell collecting, or rock collecting can encourage you to explore one area in more depth. As you learn more details about your special interest, you may find there is even more insight to gain.
- Plan a vacation that includes a natural wonder you rarely see— geysers, hot springs, caves, mountains, waterfalls, canyons, icebergs, or oceans.
- If it's possible where you live, hang a birdbath or have a bird-feeder this winter—or any time of year—and keep it filled. Keep a log of the birds that visit.
- Eat outside whenever possible. Pile on a sweater or coat in the fall. Throw a blanket on the ground if you don't have a picnic table.
- Open the windows in your house when weather permits. Roll down the windows of your car.
- Leave the house a few degrees cooler in winter and a few degrees warmer in summer to get more in tune with what's happening outside the house. Unnaturally high or low indoor temperatures from heaters and air conditioners can give us a false sense of security, making us forget our very real dependence on God.
- Admire your family, your precious children, in their beauty and

complexity. Gaze upon a sleeping baby. Marvel at a young swimmer diving into the pool. God created mankind. And it was good.

Exploring Nature in Scripture

Check out the following passages. How intimately do you know the subject matter listed in the scripture? For example, would literally "going" to the ant and considering its ways help you be wiser? Use this as a provocative study by selecting one verse that stands out to you and researching some nature study to enhance your understanding of the passage.

A Time to Reflect

Go to the ant, you sluggard; consider its ways and be wise! (Proverbs 6:6)

But his delight is in the law of the LORD, and on his law he meditates day and night. He is like a tree planted by streams of water, which yields its fruit in season and whose leaf does not wither. (Psalm 1:2-3)

[B]ut those who hope in the LORD will renew their strength. They will soar on wings like eagles. (Isaiah 40:31)

As for man, his days are like grass, he flourishes like a flower of the field; the wind blows over it and it is gone, and its place remembers it no more. (Psalm 103:15-16)

Like the coolness of snow at harvest time is a trustworthy messenger to those who send him; he refreshes the spirit of his masters. (Proverbs 25:13)

Like clouds and wind without rain is a man who boasts of gifts he does not give. (Proverbs 25:14)

There are three things that are never satisfied, four that never say, "Enough!": the grave, the barren womb, land, which is never satisfied with water, and fire, which never says, "Enough!" (Proverbs 30:15-16)

There are three things that are too amazing for me, four that I do not understand: the way of an eagle in the sky, the way of a snake on a rock, the way of a ship on the high seas, and the way of a man with a maiden. (Proverbs 30:18-19)

Four things on earth are small, yet they are extremely wise: Ants are creatures of little strength, yet they store up their food in the summer; coneys are creatures of little power, yet they make their home in the crags; locusts have no king, yet they advance together in ranks; a lizard can be caught with the hand, yet it is found in kings' palaces. (Proverbs 30:24-28)

Look at the birds of the air; they do not sow or reap or store away in barns, and yet your heavenly Father feeds them. (Matthew 6:26)

And why do you worry about clothes? See how the lilies of the field grow. They do not labor or spin. Yet I tell you that not even Solomon in all his splendor was dressed like one of these. (Matthew 6:28-29)

The kingdom of heaven is like a mustard seed, which a man took and planted in his field. Though it is the smallest of all your seeds, yet when it grows, it is the largest of garden plants and becomes a tree, so that the birds of the air come and perch in its branches. (Matthew 13:31-32; also found in Mark 4:30-32)

The kingdom of heaven is like yeast that a woman took and mixed into a large amount of flour until it worked all through the dough. (Matthew 13:33)

Now learn this lesson from the fig tree: As soon as its twigs get tender and its leaves come out, you know that summer is near.... [W]hen you see these things happening, you know that it is near, right at the door. (Mark 13:28-29)

I am the vine; you are the branches. If a man remains in me and I in him, he will bear much fruit; apart from me you can do nothing. (John 15:5)

Then the LORD God provided a vine and made it grow up over Jonah to give shade for his head to ease his discomfort, and Jonah was very happy about the vine. But at dawn the next day God provided a worm, which chewed the vine so that it withered. (Jonah 4:6-7)

Psalm 104

Psalm 148

Job 38-41

Song of Songs

Parable of the Sower, Matthew 13:3-9,18-23; Mark 4:3-9; Luke 8:5-15

Parable of the Weeds, Matthew 13:24-30

Parable of the Net, Matthew 13:47-51

Parable of the Growing Seed, Mark 4:26-29

MOMS SPEAK OUT

Kathy: When we think about what really moves our souls, it isn't usually the Empire State Building; it's Niagara Falls. It's not a dam; it's the ocean. It's all the things that *God* has made.

Debbie: I know several deeply wounded people who absolutely cannot look at a flower, a bird, a kitten, or a sunset and find it lovely or even just enjoy it. Upon that observation and other similar things (including positive ones), I've concluded that the connection to observing, admiring, and taking in God's creation is a piece of the worship of Him.

Lynn: When I'm skiing, I love to pray through Scripture verses about His awesome creation. Or when I'm backpacking, I picture Jesus sitting on top of a distant mountain and sing praises to Him as if He's there, in the flesh, waving to me. Then I picture Him walking right beside me, holding my hand as I stumble up the mountain path. This helps me picture God as He truly is—majestic and huge. He could sit on that mountain like it's a pebble, and yet He's still so interested in me that He'll walk beside me and hold my hand when I need help taking the next step.

Trish: My daughter, Sabrina, helps me see the majestic in the mundane. We were walking up to the post office to mail some presents, and I couldn't wait for vacation, to get to the mountains and get some good-looking scenery. I was focused far ahead and not on the present. As Sabrina was walking up, she gasped and said in a hushed voice,

"Mommy, look! There's a sea of *diamonds!*" This was a revelation to me. I started noticing, and you know, the glistening snow really *is* a sea of diamonds! What a blessing to have this child in my life; I would never have seen it otherwise.

Linda Z.: It's funny; when they're inside, the kids can be bickering, and then they go outside, and all of a sudden they're getting along. We've realized since we moved to the house we have now, which has more land, that we do more as a family: We play as a family, we work in the yard as a family, we feel kind of like we're out on a farm. That has helped our family dynamic a lot. We feel more unity because we go outside and play together. Steve and I both have really great memories of playing outside as kids, and we want that for our kids. There's something really healthy about getting outside and giggling and getting thrown in the dirt.

Beth: When I saw Niagara Falls, I burst into tears. I'd never been there until my husband, Jeff, took me three years ago. I had a sense I wanted to fall flat on my face. We have connected with God so many times through nature and its reflection of who God is. The diversity and creativity: The desert is so different from the ocean; the mountains are so different from the valleys. He created all these things that are *so different.* But when I went to Niagara Falls, the thing that struck me is that it's still moving. Mountains are lovely, but they just stand there. The ocean is moving, but it seems kind of "out there." But I sensed God's power more than ever before at the Falls. The ground shakes and trembles when you're standing there. If Niagara Falls is this powerful and created by God, how much more powerful is He! All it takes is His breath, and He has the right and ability to destroy or crush us at any time, yet He chooses not to because He loves us. To this day, three years later, talking about it makes me very emotional.

Susan M.: Most of my times with God occur outdoors. Sometimes I'll be out running, and I'll look up and see the stars, and it makes me think of God and how much He loves me. Or I'll get to see the sunrise, and so I use that as prayer time.

Sonya: I feel very intimidated to have a time of solitude with a roof over my head, but it changes completely when I go outside, whether it's just going on a walk or going camping on my own. Once there is no roof and there are no people, then I feel as if there are no boundaries between God and me. I think there really is something to getting rid of the manmade things that are available to our eyes, even if it is just a simple roof over our heads. There's something about seeing the sky— whether it's cloudy or starry—that kind of removes the barriers, and you can just commune in that *real* way: "Wow, you're *God!*"

Susan M.: Whenever I'm in nature, I connect with God. No wonder worship at church feels so artificial to me sometimes. We were driving to West Virginia, and even though the kids were in the back fighting, I looked at these orange, red, and yellow trees, and I thought, "Oh, God, You *made* these!" I started to bawl because all of a sudden I felt overwhelmed with a passion toward God that I rarely feel living in the suburbs.

Sonya: Part of enjoying creation is to learn more about it. You can never learn so much that you can't see more of God's design and of His holding things together. Allowing science to bring to life God's attention to detail and His great unfathomable wisdom is a cool thing I hope to learn about as my kids are learning more. However, don't let science numb you to the awe of creation. When my nephew's great-grandmother died, he said to my sister, "Mommy, how does God keep spinning the world while He's holding Grammy?" We can't miss the truth that God really is literally holding all things together, and we can't let science keep us from enjoying the truth of that.

Linda B: We went camping this year and the car ride was horrendous, but once we got there it was a common denominator.... There was something for everybody. It wasn't very comfortable or luxurious. We didn't even have showers that time. But it brought us together.

Lisa: I grew up on a farm. Some of my sweetest memories of those years are running around our property in my yellow sweatshirt and overalls, picking pears or apples at my leisure. I loved rolling on the grass and wrestling with my dog and kittens. What adventures I'd have back near the chicken coop. It's amazing how quickly you can build a stage for a circus with meager cinder blocks and plywood. Do you know how much fun it is to throw walnuts into an open field?

Experiencing Community

[Y]ou are no longer foreigners and aliens, but fellow citizens with God's people and members of God's household, built on the foundation of the apostles and prophets, with Christ Jesus himself as the chief cornerstone. In him the whole building is joined together and rises to become a holy temple in the Lord. And in him you too are being built together to become a dwelling in which God lives by his Spirit.

EPHESIANS 2:19-22

So far, contemplative "mom-hood" has for the most part been a solitary effort. Investing in your personal relationship with the Lord, you have focused your efforts and attention exclusively on Him.

As our rich relationship with God deepens, however, we'll find that He doesn't want us to keep the tingle and thrill of knowing Him to ourselves. Rather, He wants us to pass it along as we serve and love the people He puts in our lives. In fact, He often reveals Himself to others through us, as well as revealing Himself to us through others.

There's been a lot of talk about community lately. Visitors often informally evaluate a church by how much (or how little) community they experienced there. In fact, that may be a big motivation for so many churches to call their small groups and Bible studies "community groups." There's even been a trend over the last decade to call independent, nondenominational churches "community churches"—not only to connect the church to the surrounding town or city, but also to imply that the church will be a source of community for individuals who attend. It seems everybody wants community, but few people have it.

For our purposes, when I say "community" I'm referring to safe places and safe people in your life. People who know you and are known by you, people who are committed to you and who will stand by you through anything, people you call when your life—or theirs— is falling apart or exploding in joy. That definition may describe a community you don't yet have but are desperately searching for. Or maybe you already have one or two places of true community. If so, consider yourself blessed.

Sadly, you'll clearly realize what community is when you thought you had it—and discover you don't. You may have faced struggles already that have tested your sense of community, only to find that the relationships you'd counted on have failed. People may have left you, perhaps even family members. That is not God's plan; it grieves Him deeply.

The depth of any commitment is stretched and revealed in the face of such things as long-term illness or emotional blows. While we are learning more about our own dependency on God during such times—while we are struggling to stick things out with Him—we also need people who will walk through anything with us. And for Christ's sake, we need to be willing—by His empowerment—to walk with others through anything. Community costs.

CREATING COMMUNITY

" 'There are two things we cannot do alone,' says Paul Tournier. 'One is to be married and the other is to be a Christian.' "[1] We weren't meant to be alone. We were made for community—in all areas of our lives. Let's look at four of the most important in a mother's life: family community, marriage community, "moms" community, and church community.

Family Community

Our very calling in life as mothers automatically places us in the community of our families. This is a good place to start, because we need to get these relationships right in order to branch out from a healthy base to others in the world around us.

"Love begins at home," Mother Teresa claimed. "Only when love abides at home can we share it with our next-door neighbor. Then it will show forth and you will be able to say to them, 'Yes, love is here.' And then you will be able to share it with everyone around you."[2]

Let's begin with the nucleus community God has given us in our families: spouses, children, perhaps others who live under our roofs and are under our influence and care. This is where we must first get community right, loving and serving each other as Christ loves the church. As believers we should be characterized as deeply devoted in love to each other; as committed to creating a "safe place" for knowing and being known; as willing—even enthusiastic—to walk with each other through anything. Those who are empowered by Christ have access to supernatural resources to form an unshakable community.

When we do all worship the same God, we have the joy of celebrating the Lord together, holding each other accountable to similar goals, discussing the Bible together, and praying and struggling through difficulties with shared hope and faith in His sovereignty.

The most straining circumstances our family has gone through happened the summer of 1997 when my husband, Philippe, required emergency heart surgery. The day after we flew to Belgium for a family reunion and wedding, Philippe became so ill he almost died. Even as our personal drama was unfolding in hospital ICUs and postsurgical recovery rooms, this emotional and physical trauma brought Philippe and me closer to each other, our children, and also to our extended family. We realize in retrospect that the ordeal has continued to intensify and solidify our family community.

I was staying with Philippe's folks during that time, and his siblings and their families were close by as well. Because we are all believers, we could pray and struggle through with hope and faith in God's sovereignty. We had to be willing to accept whatever the outcome, which was a hard reality given the very real possibility of death.

The Lord kept us strong, and He was gracious; Philippe survived, and today is healthy. I would never have requested that emergency to happen, but I wouldn't trade the rich relationships and strong family community that have resulted for anything.

A simpler example of how our family's shared faith is helpful to building community is demonstrated by our family's prayer tin. I hope I don't trivialize the point by referring to this small thing—small as it is, it's important in our family life. Our prayer tin sits on the window ledge filled with names of people we love. Sometime during or after a family meal, we often pluck one or two names from the tin and pray together for family and friends. It's a way to honor the fact that we all are praying to the same God, believing that He is hearing our prayers and acting on them.

Of course the ideal—that everyone in the family is a follower of Christ—is not necessarily the case. But even if you are the only believer in your household, God wants your entire family to be close. You don't need a prayer tin to be close, and the Lord wants to help you go through equally difficult times as ours—or worse—and become closer than ever. Everyday acts of love build a foundation to prepare us for greater challenges. Deep bonds of love are built over time, in sickness and in health, and it is through those bonds of love that Christ is revealed.

Anita Hopper, one of the women quoted throughout this book, has maintained close ties with her grown sons despite the fact that not all of them are fellow believers in Jesus Christ. "We are so close though," she says, "and we have such a great time together." This closeness is the result of years of investing in her family. Anita recalled a time when her oldest son, Jeff, was about twelve years old. "He liked me to sit with him while he played the piano," Anita explained. "I can remember one day being so caught up in laundry, dishes, and all the stuff that I needed to get done and hearing him say from the other room, 'Mom, can you come in here and sing with me?' I remember looking at the towel I was folding, thinking, 'You know what, this towel is not important. I need to put this down and go in there and sit with him.' That little thing was a turning point in me, in my saying, 'You know, I need to love him and put him first.'"

Community is hard work, requiring us to develop a rich relationship with God that sensitizes us to His lead in situations like Anita's. That choice was the first of hundreds that built the depth of relationship and love she shares with her sons to this day.

Regardless of a family's spiritual status, community can also just be plain fun. Family game night, summer vacations, weekly dinners, and seasonal traditions are all great ways to grow close, intentionally promoting family "culture."

Do you have a family or two you look to as a model or ideal? We have several, one of which is the Day family. They are one of the closest families I know. Each member of that family is deeply devoted to the others. If one of them is in trouble, they'll cram as many Days as possible into a van or two and drive halfway across the country to be together and support each other. They laugh together and call each other by multiple nicknames ("Brother Siefert," "Myrtle," "Heidi-Ho," and "Brown Cow," to name a few). They celebrate birthdays with energy and affection, and they have been great at developing family traditions, some serious, many lighthearted.

The Days have created holiday traditions that exceed the ordinary. For example, to minimize the post-Christmas blues, "The Good King" comes on New Year's Eve, filling the kids' shoes (set outside their bedroom doors) with candy, nuts, and a little present. My personal favorite is the St. Valentine Day "Red Kangaroo," who secretly drops off red "stuff" on February 14. "The Green Leprechaun" leaves green goodies on St. Patrick's Day. For a while they even had Uncle Sam drop off red-white-and-blue surprises on the Fourth of July.

These events may not seem like much—they certainly don't cost much—but they are part of the rhythm of life with the Days and provide a sense of togetherness. Knowing which daughter is "Myrtle" and setting a shoe outside your door in anticipation of the Green Leprechaun provide an affectionate atmosphere of community that reinforces the actual community, proven each time a van takes off to support a Day in need.

We don't have nicknames in our family, but the Days have inspired us as we create our own traditions. We hate to plagiarize them, but the Days are a family to emulate in many ways. So I must admit, I have been tempted each year to have a Red Kangaroo leap through late on February 13 and leave some surprises outside the bedroom doors!

Instead, our own family "culture" reflects Philippe's and my personalities, and I guess we're a bit calmer than the Days. We do have some traditions (though they may be more like "distinguishing characteristics") that reflect our preferences: We eat crepes for dinner on Sunday nights and camp each spring in Florida. We love Chinese food, going barefoot, and *The Little Princess*. Lately we've been dancing to mambo music before and after dinner. These things—most of which were not planned in advance to become traditions—have provided a sense of togetherness.

Some of our friends are much classier than we are. They host fancy tea parties for their daughters and enjoy stylish evenings dining on fine china and silver. They create their own memorable mood that instills a sense of fun quite different from our barefoot mambo-dancing scene but is equally powerful in tying them together.

Whether you're kooky or classy, capitalize on your personality and style to build lifelong bonds and a loving support system that God can use to draw your family together.

Our personal focus on Christ will have a powerful effect on our families. As Christ changes us, molds us, and moves in us, He will directly impact our families through us. While our focus should remain on Christ Himself—not on the idea that we are modeling a walk with God—there still may be moments when we can teach a principle to our children or offer encouragement to our spouse. In the long run, though, God Himself will do what needs to be done in the hearts and souls of our families. Our best bet is to stay close to Christ and let Him create the intimate family community He desires for us.

Marriage Community

If you're married, the most critical relationship in your family—and the most critical relationship in your life outside your relationship with God—is with your spouse.

Community in marriage is the most intimate of all human relationships. It models—imperfectly, of course, because of sin—the relationship we have with God through Christ. In Scripture He has given us the marriage relationship as a way to grasp His passionate commitment to His bride, "the church." Thus, even our children will get their first concepts of how God loves the church—and them—by observing healthy marriages. We, too, will gain insight into how God loves the church as we experience the mystery and challenges of marriage. When we appreciate and understand the community, commitment, and intimacy that take place within marriage, we will more fully appreciate the community, commitment, and intimacy that Christ offers us.

We need to take steps to comprehend God's perfect plan for marriage and to preserve and protect our marriages, not only because they are educational settings to learn about our great God (and to learn about our own sinfulness and need for a Savior), but also because marriage has intrinsic value as two people in ultimate community on earth. God desires for us to pursue, by His grace, His perfect design for marriage.

Marriage community deserves every erg of energy we can give to keep it strong and push it closer to God's ideal. Study Scripture, and invest in books or marriage seminars that will provide you with professional resources. Your marriage is about much more than you may realize. Make it a priority to pursue community in your partnership as long as you both shall live.

This time I'm not going to give you a list of ideas for ways to strengthen your marriage; compared to the importance and depth of the marriage community, any ideas I might offer here could appear trite. I have included a section on marriage resources in the appendix. Check them against what your own leaders suggest; your church and pastor need to lead you in this area. Ask them for recommendations on books on marriage for you and your husband to study together. Also ask about marriage conferences and seminars, Bible studies at your church that focus on marriage, older couples who might be marriage mentors for you, tapes on marriage you can order, and counselors, if you are facing more serious struggles.

"Moms" Community

What does a mom do without a network of fellow moms? For me, the early years of motherhood prompted urgent, pressing questions about everything from when to start solid foods and potty training to how I should organize stuffed animals and keep track of dozens of microscopic Playmobil parts. The questions don't stop as the children grow either. They just shift focus: from monitoring your baby's every sound to monitoring your sixth grader's use of the Internet; from wondering when is too early for your daughter to start wearing makeup to when is too late for her to stay out after the prom.

Recently I interviewed a group of women for this book, and as soon as we gathered under the same roof, we naturally broke off into small groups based on the ages of our children. Moms with young kids started comparing grade school problems while moms with older kids instantly fell into discussions about their sons' and daughters' dating dilemmas.

Spending that evening together revealed something to all of us: We need women in our lives—fellow moms, both peers and mentors—to bounce off every issue of motherhood. We need women we know are dedicated to helping us stay close to Christ: to hold us accountable to our goals; to pray with us about our concerns; and to dig into our lives, walking with us through dark times, self-doubt, and confusion. And we need a network of moms who will, in an emergency, take our kids at a moment's notice.

If you don't yet have a small community of moms to turn to, there are places to look while you pray and wait for the women God has chosen for you. "Formal" settings might include Bible studies or mom-support groups like MOPS (Mothers of Preschoolers) or Moms in Touch; these are great places to meet like-minded women with kids of similar ages. You might also meet other moms at planned neighborhood activities like block parties. Check out playgroups, too. If you teach at home, contact a home-school support group. You might even start a neighborhood Bible study or book club in your home. These are all fun settings from which a committed friendship may spring forth and take root in your life.

Moms interact informally, too, of course. I've met neighbors in the backyard while taking a break from raking leaves. School functions and PTA meetings, soccer meets and gymnastics classes are natural places to meet other moms.

Your impact as a believer in these places is also crucial to God's kingdom. Your intimate relationship with the God of the universe lived out honestly among these women will serve as inspiration. Don't be surprised if you start getting questions about what keeps you calm, peaceful, or strong.

If you live in an isolated area or aren't finding people locally and feel desperate for immediate input and support, a secondary source of community can be found on the Internet. For me, one of the best uses of an e-mail community is maintaining existing friendships with women who have moved away. But you can also meet moms around the world on the Internet and develop a "virtual" community of women in chat rooms, on message boards, and within interest groups.

This kind of community can be deceptive though. It's easy to think your e-friendships are deeper than they really are, so I'd suggest viewing any on-line community as down a notch from a community of real-life, flesh-and-blood women whose sliding glass doors your kids have smudged and whose chocolate-chip cookies you have devoured.

In spite of that caveat, one excellent use of the Internet is for moms to find other moms dealing with delicate or specialized issues. In these cases, a degree of anonymity or a limited depth of relationship might come in handy. A friend of mine who has adopted a child with a mental handicap has been thrilled to find other moms on-line with similar struggles who offer suggestions.

Finally, back to real-time, off-line relationships—don't neglect getting together with established friends for lunch or late-night coffee breaks. Occasionally I can manage to have someone over to my home midmorning or in the afternoon for tea, but I'm not genteel enough to make it a regular event. The important thing is to maintain regular contact with fellow moms to whom you are already committed and who are committed to you.

God seems to have wired into us this emotional instinct to need female friendships. Don't fight it. Let God lead you to like-minded women, whether informally or formally. Giggle and cry with them. Take notes on how to manage computer time with two teenagers in the house. Give someone your tips on organizing lunchboxes for a school day. Swap ideas for getting time alone with God (and mail them to me while you're at it!). We're all in this together, and God knows it. He gave us each other for a reason. We don't have to get through this alone.

Church Community

Years ago I heard author Maxine Hancock, now a professor at Regent College in Vancouver, British Columbia, speak at a writers' conference. At that time she lived near a small town in Alberta, Canada, where there was one church in town. One. No chance for church hopping there. Like it or not, that was her family's church. If she had a falling out with someone, she couldn't walk away. She had no choice but to stay and work it out.

That is how Hancock prefaced an analogy that has stuck with me for years. I have her permission to paraphrase the analogy from memory:

We're like rocks in a rock polisher. A rock goes into the rock polisher all rocklike, dark and not particularly attractive. Then all the other rocks start knocking against it, hitting it, chipping off pieces here and there. It's hard to believe that all of that jostling is doing any good. But after a long process—weeks or even months later—you open up the rock polisher, reach in, and pull out a spectacular, gleaming stone!

"Invest yourself in one group of people, one church," Hancock proposed in her talk, "and see what impact you can have on one another, over the years, as Christ moves in and through you to polish you into glorious creations conformed to Christ."

Glorious creations conformed to Christ! Can we do that for each other? Can even our mistakes be used to polish others? How about in good ways? Can we influence people so powerfully through love that we are part of their maturity process?

Not only can we, we must. We are to be, in the church and in each other's lives, exercising such extraordinary love and commitment to each other that people who aren't believers will exclaim, "Look at the way they love! You sure don't see that every day! They must be disciples of Jesus Christ!" (cf. John 13:35).

Christ has called us to a radical, new community that loves to a degree no other community on earth is capable of except by His empowerment. We are to be committed to the people in our church community—wholly devoted to them, both in their righteous moments and their sinful slumps, both when we understand them and when we're upset by them. We are to pour ourselves sacrificially into the lives of fellow believers. This is why God gave us gifts: to serve the body of Christ.

And the body of Christ has a job: God's intent was that the church would be the means by which the wisdom of God would be revealed (see Ephesians 3:10). The church can only do this when we all walk humbly with the Lord, serving each other with our gifts, looking after the needs of others as well as ourselves, and seeking God's will above all else.

As part of the church, we individual moms need to make every effort to keep the unity of the Spirit in the churches we're involved in. That's what it says in Romans 14:19, Ephesians 4:3, and Hebrews 12:14, too. Make every effort. Make every effort to do what leads to peace and mutual edification, to keep the unity of the Spirit through the bond of peace, to live in peace with everyone.

Make every effort? That sounds tiring. That sounds like a stretch. That sounds like we'll have to go above and beyond the call of duty. That doesn't sound like what the world says. The world says, "Aw, it isn't worth the effort. You've given them enough of your time and energy. It's too hard. If there's nothing in it for you anymore, just move on." God, however, says, "Make every effort." It is worth the effort. This is it! If we don't make every effort to keep unity among ourselves, the church won't fulfill one of its primary callings: to reveal God. This is the plan, so make every effort to enable the church to be God's loud-speaker to the rulers and authorities in the heavenly realms and on earth. Make every effort to keep peace with all men and women. The kingdom is counting on you.

In her book *Re-evaluating Your Commitments,* Maxine Hancock quotes John Stott: "The Christian life is not just our own private affair.... It is no good supposing that membership of the universal church of Christ is enough; we must belong to some local branch of it.... Every Christian's place is in a local church, sharing in its worship, its fellowship and its witness."[3]

Take the plunge into the rock polisher of your church, and start tumbling around with those people, imperfect and rocklike as they may be. It's called community. Sometimes it feels like a fun, twirling ride; other times it feels like a painful collision, and we end up in emotional traction as a result. I pray God gives us the courage to stick it out with the same bunch of rocks—working through the difficulties by His grace. God can make something beautiful even from the pain we cause each other, redeeming it by using it as a transforming force in our lives.

The apostle Paul offers practical advice in many of the epistles for how brothers and sisters in Christ are to work through their struggles and live together in harmony, serving God together. Read through them, and you'll find that by God's empowerment we may have to lay down our lives, our pride, our feelings, our preferences, and our need to be understood in order to promote unity in the body.

As you gently pursue deeper commitment to people, some may resist, preferring their walls of self-protection. Our definition of community—a place where we can safely both know others and be known, a place where we expect others to stand by us through everything and expect ourselves to do the same for them—may overwhelm people in this isolationist culture. Many people, while pleasant and often quite open about some things in their lives, seem to fear authentic intimacy and commitment. Maybe the idea of true community overwhelms even you. Be patient. Don't force it—but don't give up either. Worship the Lord, and love His people with all you've got. Pray. And wait for God's promptings to learn how to love well.

SUSTAINING COMMUNITY

The church isn't the only place where the rock polisher analogy applies. The fact is that for all our efforts to pursue community in our churches and with our families and friends, whenever a group of human beings lives, serves, and works together, there will be relational difficulties. It doesn't matter who it is; conflict, friction, and pain are unavoidable if community is to be significant and long-term. Like the grinding of rocks against each other in the polisher, it's part of the process of transformation.

The question, then, isn't whether or not difficulties exist among us. The question is how we will handle them. More specifically, "How will I, personally, handle them?" When problems arise in our families or churches, when conflicts come up between friends, when unity seems more a pipe dream than a possibility—what will we do? What can we do?

Practicing Unity

I believe we must first acknowledge our need for each other. We need those safe places—beyond the secret place we have with God—to know and to be known: our family, our marriage, our friendships, our church. As followers of Christ we also need each other simply to survive in a postmodern culture that is apathetic, if not downright antagonistic, toward our belief system. In unity lies safety and strength.

We must understand the significance of our unity as well. In our oneness with other believers, we represent the Bride of Christ. Jesus' passionate love for us individually is only a taste of His passionate love for us as the church. He has given us to each other and called us to unity with each other that we might experience unity with Him. We're talking about something huge here, a richness with Christ beyond anything we can conceive.

Christ hasn't left us to our own devices as far as making this unity happen either. Because He is in us, He can empower us to radically embrace His dream—the dream of new life in a new community of united believers. Unity with other believers—supernatural, mind-boggling unity—is possible because Christ hoped for it, commanded it, prayed for it, preached it, and died for it. It truly can happen.

So, in order to promote unity in the church and among our friends and family members, we must accept responsibility for doing our part to practice it.

I know a woman of God who lies in bed each night and reviews every minute detail of her day—evaluates it and asks God if she has offended anyone. If *anything* comes up in this review, even something minor, she goes the very next morning to deal with it, face to face if at all possible.

This woman lives at a very practical level the advice from Hebrews:

"Make every effort to live in peace with all men and to be holy.... See to it that no one misses the grace of God and that no bitter root grows up to cause trouble and defile many" (12:14-15). She addresses potential problems as soon as possible to avoid letting a bitter root grow up in someone else. During her nightly review, she also lets go of any bitterness she herself might be holding on to, often overlooking an offense. "He who covers over an offense promotes love, but whoever repeats the matter separates close friends" (Proverbs 17:9). "A man's wisdom gives him patience; it is to his glory to overlook an offense" (Proverbs 19:11).

You know what? We owe it to each other to follow the example of this woman. Our unity as believers depends on it—and our unity with Christ. If someone offends me and I let bitterness creep into my heart, if I clench it for dear life, I will spoil the church. I will "defile the many." And I will grieve my Lord. Sometimes I need to let go when I am offended. Overlook it. Cover it up. Forget about it. Other times I will need to talk face to face with someone to clear up things. But bitterness has no place in me. It has no place in the church.

More than anything, as followers of Christ we ought to "love each other deeply, because love covers over a multitude of sins" (1 Peter 4:8). Jesus Christ Himself can flow through us and empower us to love when we've been wronged. The church is dying for this kind of radical response to offenses. To be a true community, we must practice love. We must practice unity.

The following prayer is one of my favorite passages of Scripture, in part I think because I love "the church"—and my church in particular—so much, and I hold out hope for us all to "get it right." So did the Lord Jesus Christ:

> My prayer is not for them [the disciples] alone. I pray also for those who will believe in me through their message, that all

of them may be one, Father, just as you are in me and I am in you. May they also be in us so that the world may believe that you have sent me. I have given them the glory that you gave me, that they may be one as we are one: I in them and you in me. May they be brought to complete unity to let the world know that you sent me and have loved them even as you have loved me. (John 17:20-23)

Let's pray with Jesus the Christ for unity among believers. Let's allow Him to use us as peacemakers. It is His dream that we—His church, His Bride—will share such unity of purpose and love that through it the world will believe in the Father who sent Him. "[S]o in Christ we who are many form one body, *and each member belongs to all the others*" (Romans 12:5, emphasis mine). What a beautiful image— what a beautiful reality! We belong to Christ. We belong to His church.

We belong to each other.

A Time to Reflect

God gives us principles in His Word for practicing unity. Review the following verses, asking Him to show you what you can do to promote growth and healing within your community relationships. Then ask Him to empower you to follow through.

For where two or three come together in my name, there am I with them. (Matthew 18:20)

Therefore encourage one another and build each other up, just as in fact you are doing. (1 Thessalonians 5:11)

There is neither Jew nor Greek, slave nor free, male nor female, for you are all one in Christ Jesus. (Galatians 3:28)

Be completely humble and gentle; be patient, bearing with one another in love. Make every effort to keep the unity of the Spirit through the bond of peace. There is one body and one Spirit—just as you were called to one hope when you were called—one Lord, one faith, one baptism; one God and Father of all, who is over all and through all and in all. (Ephesians 4:2-6)

[S]erve one another in love. The entire law is summed up in a single command: "Love your neighbor as yourself." If you keep on biting and devouring each other, watch out or you will be destroyed by each other. (Galatians 5:13-15)

[L]et us do good to all people, especially to those who belong to the family of believers. (Galatians 6:10)

The end of all things is near. Therefore be clear minded and self-controlled so that you can pray. Above all, love each other deeply, because love covers over a multitude of sins. (1 Peter 4:7-8)

Now that you have purified yourselves by obeying the truth so that you have sincere love for your brothers, love one another deeply, from the heart. (1 Peter 1:22)

May the Lord make your love increase and overflow for each other. (1 Thessalonians 3:12)

Therefore each of you must put off falsehood and speak truthfully to his neighbor, for we are all members of one body. (Ephesians 4:25)

"In your anger do not sin": Do not let the sun go down while you are still angry. (Ephesians 4:26)

Submit to one another out of reverence for Christ.
(Ephesians 5:21)

Show proper respect to everyone: Love the brotherhood of
believers, fear God, honor the king. (1 Peter 2:17)

Let the peace of Christ rule in your hearts, since as members
of one body you were called to peace. And be thankful. Let
the word of Christ dwell in you richly as you teach and
admonish one another with all wisdom, and as you sing
psalms, hymns and spiritual songs with gratitude in your
hearts to God. (Colossians 3:15-16)

Love must be sincere. Hate what is evil; cling to what is
good. Be devoted to one another in brotherly love. Honor
one another above yourselves.... Be joyful in hope, patient in
affliction, faithful in prayer. Share with God's people who are
in need. Practice hospitality. (Romans 12:9-10,12-13)

Bless those who persecute you; bless and do not curse.
Rejoice with those who rejoice; mourn with those who
mourn. Live in harmony with one another. Do not be proud,
but be willing to associate with people of low position. Do
not be conceited. (Romans 12:14-16)

Do not repay anyone evil for evil. Be careful to do what is
right in the eyes of everybody. If it is possible, as far as it
depends on you, live at peace with everyone. Do not take
revenge, my friends, but leave room for God's wrath, for it is
written: "It is mine to avenge; I will repay," says the Lord.
(Romans 12:17-19)

Therefore confess your sins to each other and pray for each
other so that you may be healed. (James 5:16)

And let us consider how we may spur one another on toward love and good deeds. Let us not give up meeting together, as some are in the habit of doing, but let us encourage one another—and all the more as you see the Day approaching. (Hebrews 10:24-25)

[M]ake my joy complete by being like-minded, having the same love, being one in spirit and purpose. Do nothing out of selfish ambition or vain conceit, but in humility consider others better than yourselves. Each of you should look not only to your own interests, but also to the interests of others. (Philippians 2:2-4)

Creating Community Traditions

Personal and community traditions can open our hearts to others and help us see how we belong in and contribute to the body of Christ. Here are some ideas for creating traditions that can move you toward healing when you've been hurt or lay a strong foundation of symbolic reminders of what community is all about. Let these suggestions ignite your imagination to create some traditions of your own.

- Mix a collection of polished and unpolished stones in a bowl as a visual reminder of our current unfinished state. (Read 1 Peter 2:4-8 or Ephesians 2:19-22, and discover how we are living stones built into a spiritual house.)
- Buy or borrow a rock polisher. Run it each Sunday with your family or during a small group meeting. Start a collection of polished stones, adding to it regularly and thanking God each time for what He is doing in your lives. Read Revelation 21:3-4, and imagine the day we'll all be gleaming and polished. In the meantime, ask God to minimize the friction we cause each other.

- Plan a monthly or seasonal family foot-washing ceremony.
  Read John 13:1-20, then pair up family members with small
  tubs of warm water. Put on some worship music, and pull out
  some soaps, oils, and lotions to use while serving each other in
  this tangible, humbling way. (Do this in a church community
  if you feel daring. It could be a powerful event.)
- Hold a confession service specifically to give people a chance to
  write out and tack onto a cross their sins against people in that
  very community, whether family, small group, or entire church.
  Give them an opportunity to ask forgiveness of the people, as
  well as the Lord. Read James 5:16, or post it for everyone to
  see. Pull down the sins and burn them in a fireproof container.
- Design a personal "Year of Jubilee" ceremony in which you
  cancel all debts and sins committed against you (see Leviticus
  25). Let Christ help you release everything you've been harbor-
  ing, even if the people responsible never ask forgiveness. You
  might buy one helium balloon to represent each person or
  event you struggle with. Release them at the end, symbolic of
  the supernatural release Christ can do.
- Celebrate events on the church calendar with circles of believers, incorporating ancient traditions with contemporary ideas
  of your own.
- I know it sounds simple, but never underestimate the impact
  of a "group hug."
- Choose several hymns that will be your family's repertoire. Sing
  them throughout the day, including the Doxology at dinner-
  time. These hymns of faith will "belong" to you.
- Tell stories and read classic literature aloud. This will give you a
  common body of material to refer to that will bind you together.
- Laugh. A lot. Bring joy into your family or church experience.
- Do the same thing every Saturday morning (it could be

anything: Eat pancakes first, then go for a hike at a park, return, and together clean the entire house).

- Invent mealtime traditions. Saying grace is an obvious one. Serving tea or coffee and lingering together afterward—even when there's no company—is another.

MOMS SPEAK OUT

Beth: Without Christ, Jeff and I would never have made it. In all honesty I don't know how marriages survive without sharing a relationship

---

CREATE SEASONAL TRADITIONS

Seasonal events can offer valuable opportunities to build community. Here are just a few ideas to get you started:

1. Celebrate Advent season as more than a shopping-days countdown. Make a nativity scene, go caroling in your neighborhood, bake cookies, and play Handel's *Messiah* throughout the Christmas season.

2. Commit as a group or family to fast from something during Lent. A common commitment can pull you together. (Ideas: fast from television, fast food, or bad habits. It can be healing and fun to remind each other.)

3. Follow a fun ritual on every birthday. (Ideas: Have everyone serve the birthday person breakfast in bed, have the birthday girl or guy wear a crown at dinner, and post photographs of the birthday person throughout the house.)

4. Find out the birthdays of friends or acquaintances, and come up with a personal, inexpensive birthday ritual to remember and celebrate their lives, bringing you together on their big day.

with Jesus. It has kept Jeff and me together in the hard times. And in the good times, there's nothing more affirming than sharing what's going on in our lives and what God's teaching us. I think intimacy with God definitely grows and is challenged by the successes and failures we've had in our marriage.

Rae: To me the key thing to learn with my family is to lean on the Lord and not to take the reins in my own hands and to be grateful for His timing. He brought me to Him when He chose to bring me to Him. Very early as a believer I responded, "Why so late? Why wait until my children were grown?" Within weeks I was complaining to God about His timing—how arrogant of me! But finally I learned that the Lord's timing is always perfect and He has a plan. We don't convert. We model, but we don't convert. That is the Lord's work. He does the work, and we live out our relationship with Him. It's been awesome to see what He's done in my family; it's been incredible. The thing I have tried to do with my children is to make God alive for them, to make Him seem real to them, to make them see that He cares about the little details.

Linda Z.: One of the best things I've done is to go to a weekly Bible study. That kept me in God's Word on a weekly basis, and I can look back on my life now and say, "You know for thirteen years I've done this almost every week." I feel that getting in those rich relationships with women has always given me hope and kept me close to the Lord and His Word. I have women around me who give me perspective and fellowship and love and who model Christ at all their different stages of life, marriage, and motherhood.

Beth: When my kids were young, at least a couple of times a week I would have moms over who had young kids like mine. I remember sitting on the floor with the kids all around, trying to complete a sentence. That started the first sense of community I ever had. As a mother with young children, you can often feel very isolated. I don't know if this is personality or what, but I was determined not to be an isolated person. The mistake we sometimes make is waiting for it to happen instead of just caring for people.

Trish: If you look at the Scriptures, you can't ignore those verses of loving someone—"love one another," "love your neighbor." The Scriptures keep going back over it. Love is all over the Bible. It's so easy to step away from people who hurt your feelings, but that's not what the Bible says to do.

Beth: Community is deep sharing; it's being willing to be honest and open with each other. That's what I really believe creates community. That's why you can't necessarily make it happen, because some people want to be social, but they don't necessarily want to be honest or vulnerable. I believe there's a huge difference. You can have a group that's very social and spends a lot of time together, but that's not community. I'm looking for something much different. They're having a great time studying the Word and spending time together, but their lives may be falling apart. Community for me is vulnerability and honesty in our lives together and in our relationship with Christ.

Rae: We have FFDs, "Forced Family Dinings," and we still do them around Christmastime, even though some of my kids now have families of their own. Forced Family Dinings you have to attend. The kids love each other anyway, but this is a wonderful thing we have done over the years. We try to make the times convenient and make it fun. We might all go out to pizza and then see a movie together and talk about it after. When kids get to the teenage years and get involved in their activities, it's nice to have an activity the kids, with their range of ages, can all do together. This was one of the little things we did to help develop those bonds between siblings.

Beth: I believe community is really important but should never replace God Himself. I never want to make the community be Jesus. Community is not meant to replace Him. I think community is supposed to point us back to Jesus. Obviously we are called to care and meet some of those needs with each other, but community can't replace Him. We'll never be able to meet each other's needs. Ultimately the greatest gift I can give my children—not that I ignore the needs I can meet—is to point them to Jesus.

Lisa: After four long, wrenching years of infertility, my husband and I finally conceived. I could hardly wait to tell our family and friends our good news. I knew, in fact, that many had been begging God to grant us a child at a time when we found it difficult to approach Him anymore. The rejoicing that took place after we shared the news changed my life. We felt celebrated; Jesus was loving us through those precious people. I learned though that we would have missed that joy had we never shared the heartache of childlessness with our friends and family in the first place. Community is a beautiful gift. Heartache is divided, but the joy is multiplied!

Rae: With all the little things pulling at moms, it's hard to get the order right, but it should be the Lord, the husband, then the children. Frequently it's the children who come first because they're pulling at you. I put my husband [who isn't a believer] after the Lord, but it's hard for him to understand that. I can understand why it's difficult—it would be difficult if I weren't a believer and felt I was coming second. But my husband's tenderness and humor about it have helped sustain me.

When I'm studying for a class I'll be teaching, he'll poke and tease me, but he knows it's important to me and honors that.

Barb: My dependence on the Lord helped me see that I wasn't supposed to be both mother and father to my daughters after Ron died. They needed to learn how to lean on the Lord Himself as their Father. I find myself fretting even now that they are adults about whether or not their relationship with Him is as vital as it "should be," but I can't do much about that other than model what a vital relationship looks like.

Rae: God has placed in my life very godly women, which has been critical to my growth. I think that is critical to all women's growth. The Lord says don't give up meeting together and let us encourage one another toward love and good deeds. God put me in a position to have the women of our church as part of my life. I didn't understand in the beginning how critical that was, but I can see it so clearly now.

Anita: Don and I hit a rough spot in our marriage and didn't know how to get through it. We had gotten into a big argument and were at an impasse. There was a Bible lying nearby, and all of a sudden I reached over and flipped it open to 1 Corinthians. I had no idea what I would open up to or why I would open a Bible at that time. I read 1 Corinthians 13 out loud, and then I looked at him and said, "We don't love each other." And he said, "No, we don't." We got down on our knees and asked God to help us love. That transformed our lives. It completely changed our marriage. I committed that passage to memory and began to look at people in light of that. "Is this really loving people?" God gave us the ability to love like that, to put each other before ourselves. Loving people has to be one of the biggest results of having a relationship with Christ. It doesn't make any sense if I say I love Christ but I don't love people because that's what He's all about.

A Love Like No Other

Holy, holy, holy is the Lord God Almighty, who was, and is, and is to come.

REVELATION 4:8

Our Father who art in heaven, hallowed be Thy name. "Our Father" has that familiar relational feel to it that we have been discussing at length in these pages. Thinking of God as our Father frees us to consider ourselves valued, beloved daughters in His family.

I long so much for us to know God intimately that I have purposefully used terms in this book that we normally apply to human relationships. For example, instead of talking only about prayer, meditation, or study, I referred to communication with God. Instead of camping on the word *solitude,* I chose to get us thinking about time alone with the Beloved.

I hoped to jolt our thinking out of the "doing" and into the "being with" mode. I wanted us to approach God as a living Being who passionately loves us, our Father in heaven. Instead of our becoming more religious and increasing our devotional efforts, I wanted us simply to know Him. Using terminology that made Him seem less far-off and more approachable seemed to be a way to do that.

But I fear that in our pursuit of intimacy and rich relationship with the Lord, we may lose something. We may sell God short. He may seem so much like a friend or family member that we forget to worship Him.

We may come to expect something from Him. We might even think of Him as *like* us.

God may have been tempted in every way just as we are, yet He was without sin. He is sinless, pure, holy, perfect, unchangeable, eternal. In those ways He is nothing like us. Exploring the uniqueness of God will protect us from thinking low thoughts of Him, degrading Him. In the same breath that we utter, "Our Father who art in heaven," we also say, "hallowed be Thy name." His name is to be hallowed. He is holy, sacred, and honored.

Holy, Holy, Holy

The four consonants of the ancient Hebrew name for God, often recorded as JHVH or YHWH, were considered too sacred to be spoken aloud. If the Hebrews didn't feel they could utter the name of YHWH out loud, who are we to chat with Him while we *mop?* Could God's sacredness, holiness, and hallowedness be compromised in our desire to know Him in our everyday life?

I don't mean to scare you, but people *have* been struck dead when they walked into the Lord's presence unclean. If they didn't drop dead, there was certainly no place for presumption that they were worthy to waltz into the Most Holy Place without following the Lord's precise instructions. In his book *The Knowledge of the Holy,* A. W. Tozer observes, "Wherever God appeared to men in Bible times the results were the same—an overwhelming sense of terror and dismay, a wrenching sensation of sinfulness and guilt."[1]

Isaiah saw the train of God's robe fill the temple and heard seraphs saying, "Holy, holy, holy is the LORD Almighty; the whole earth is full of his glory." The doorposts and thresholds shook, and the temple was filled with smoke. Isaiah was floored by God's holiness. "Woe to me!" he cried with that sense of terror and dismay described by Tozer. "I am ruined! For I am a man of unclean lips, and I live among a people of unclean lips, and my eyes have seen the King, the LORD Almighty" (Isaiah 6:3-5).

When Job questioned God about all that was happening in his life, the Lord answered him out of a storm. "Brace yourself like a man," the Lord commanded. "I will question you, and you shall answer me. Where were you when I laid the earth's foundation? Tell me, if you understand. Who marked off its dimensions? Surely you know!" (Job 38:3-5).

Job responded to the Lord's long list of Creator credentials in humility, "Surely I spoke of things I did not understand, things too wonderful for me to know.... My ears had heard of you but now my eyes have seen you. Therefore I despise myself and repent in dust and ashes" (Job 42:3,5-6).

There is no room for audacity on our part. The LORD, YHWH, is God, and there is no other. He is the I AM. He stands alone. He is infinite and incomprehensible. "Who has understood the mind of the LORD, or instructed him as his counselor?" (Isaiah 40:13). "'For my thoughts are not your thoughts, neither are your ways my ways,' declares the LORD. 'As the heavens are higher than the earth, so are my ways higher than your ways and my thoughts than your thoughts'" (Isaiah 55:8-9).

We cannot presume to comprehend His thoughts or ways. The LORD is so "other" than us that familiarity with God seems a tad laughable. And chumminess, well...let's not even go there. As Tozer writes, "The self-assurance of modern Christians, the basic levity present in so many of our religious gatherings, the shocking disrespect shown for the Person of God, are evidence enough of deep blindness of heart."[2]

Are we guilty of a deep blindness of heart? In our attempts to become intimate in a deepening relationship with God, are we displaying a shocking disrespect toward Him? Who am I to think that I can talk with the God of gods while I push my daughter on the swing? Who are we to think that fitting in a short prayer at a stoplight or while charging along on a power walk is acceptable? Can we ponder some eternal truth while spot cleaning the carpet and washing windows, or does that dishonor the King of kings?

Don't worry. I haven't negated the entire book in one fell swoop. We *can* do all those things. We *can* talk with God and ponder truth anywhere. But only because of Christ Jesus.

The incomprehensible God is made comprehensible through Christ Jesus our Lord. The unapproachable God is approachable only through Him—

> Who, being in very nature God,
> > did not consider equality with God something to be
> > > grasped,
> but made himself nothing,
> > taking the very nature of a servant,
> > being made in human likeness.
> And being found in appearance as a man,
> > he humbled himself
> > and became obedient to death—
> > > even death on a cross! (Philippians 2:6-8)

This truth is huge. It makes our intimacy with God even more astonishing, precious, and mind-boggling. Understanding that God Himself has made familiarity with Him possible through the blood of Jesus Christ causes me to respond in humble awe. I am not worthy. I've done nothing to deserve friendship with God. Even if I tried to earn it, "all our righteous acts are like filthy rags" (Isaiah 64:6). The fact that I have a love relationship with the Almighty God is only by His grace, through Jesus Christ His Son.

All that we have talked about in this book—the rich relationship, intimacy with God, understanding what He has to say to us, communicating with Him—all of it is possible through Jesus Christ. God first reached out to us. "[W]hile we were yet sinners, Christ died for us" (Romans 5:8, NASB). God took the risk to be known.

We *can* utter the name of God our Father—familiar and intimate—and do so in full confidence. It is with gratitude and amazement that we have access to the inaccessible. "Let us then approach the throne of grace with confidence, so that we may receive mercy and find grace to help us in our time of need" (Hebrews 4:16). Full access to the throne of grace for a sinner like me. It still floors me.

Understanding who I am in light of who God is leads me to a healthy humility and "fear." Yes, through Jesus I may confidently approach God's throne. Realizing the cost and magnitude of this privilege stirs up respect, reverence, and gratitude. I have an audience with the King of kings, any time, any day, through Christ Jesus.

I have, in fact, been in dialogue with the King regarding this very chapter. I have struggled with how to express this truth of God's holiness. Here is a recent journal entry:

You are holy. Who am I to write of holiness?

I am not worthy. It is only Jesus Christ who makes any
word that comes out of my keyboard worth reading. Save
me, Lord, from uttering anything not worthy of You.

Our Father, who art in heaven, hallowed be Thy Name.

May Your name be hallowed. Each time I say it. Whether
I am sprawled out prostrate on the ground in humble prayer,
or clattering pans in the kitchen, or changing the sheets. I am
only holy because You are holy and You give to me holiness
through the Son who indwells me by His Holy Spirit and
covers me by His blood.

Please unlock the barrier in my mind that is keeping me

from expressing this reality. Perhaps I don't grasp it enough to express it. Perhaps I have not honored You and Your "otherness" in my own life enough to humbly present it to others.

Forgive any audacity on my part that I might be worthy of putting words to this.

By God's grace through Jesus Christ, I pray any audacity on my part is gone. Now I must trust Christ to communicate clearly to you the truth about His holiness and how He has made a way.

For reasons beyond our understanding, our Creator is passionately interested in each one of us. And so as you are moving into greater intimacy with God through Jesus Christ, may you know Him in every way, revering Him as you dialogue with Him. Worshiping Him as you listen for His voice. Walking with Him as a companion, yet realizing this companion is the Holy God of Israel, the God of the universe— the one, true God.

THE HOLY GOD INCARNATE

The apostle Paul experienced God's grace and was made right with God through Jesus Christ. He knew intimacy with God. He knew about the inaccessible being made accessible. He knew that the unknowable God was knowable through Jesus.

We, too, can know God as Paul did. Meditating on His attributes—what He reveals about Himself in His Word—helps us gain an accurate picture of who He is. Check out Exodus, Job, and the prophets, for starters. The great I AM makes exclusive claims about Himself, emphasizing His holiness and His unapproachability.

Now, read the following words that Jesus said of Himself, recorded in the book of John. If some of these verses stand out to you, be sure to look them up in your own Bible to confirm the setting and the audience

Jesus was addressing. You'll understand His words much better if you know whether He was calmly teaching His disciples, exclaiming to the crowds, or standing to be condemned. There's a lot here. Spend all afternoon on it if you can. It is worth the time for you to know the LORD and His claims personally.

A Time to Reflect

The woman said, "I know that Messiah" (called Christ) "is coming. When he comes, he will explain everything to us." Then Jesus declared, "I who speak to you am he." (John 4:25-26)

I tell you the truth, the Son can do nothing by himself; he can do only what he sees his Father doing, because whatever the Father does the Son also does. (John 5:19)

By myself I can do nothing; I judge only as I hear, and my judgment is just, for I seek not to please myself but him who sent me. (John 5:30)

You diligently study the Scriptures because you think that by them you possess eternal life. These are the Scriptures that testify about me, yet you refuse to come to me to have life. (John 5:39-40)

I do not accept praise from men, but I know you. I know that you do not have the love of God in your hearts. I have come in my Father's name, and you do not accept me. (John 5:41-43)

If you believed Moses, you would believe me, for he wrote about me. (John 5:46)

I am the bread of life. He who comes to me will never go hungry, and he who believes in me will never be thirsty. (John 6:35)

For I have come down from heaven not to do my will but to do the will of him who sent me.... For my Father's will is that everyone who looks to the Son and believes in him shall have eternal life, and I will raise him up at the last day. (John 6:38,40)

I am the living bread that came down from heaven. If anyone eats of this bread, he will live forever. (John 6:51)

I am the light of the world. Whoever follows me will never walk in darkness, but will have the light of life. (John 8:12)

You are from below; I am from above. You are of this world; I am not of this world.... [I]f you do not believe that I am the one I claim to be, you will indeed die in your sins. (John 8:23-24)

I came from God and now am here. I have not come on my own; but he sent me. (John 8:42)

"I tell you the truth," Jesus answered, "before Abraham was born, I am!" (John 8:58)

[Jesus] said, "Do you believe in the Son of Man?" "Who is he, sir?" the man asked. "Tell me so that I may believe in him." Jesus said, "You have now seen him; in fact, he is the one speaking with you." (John 9:35-37)

I am the gate for the sheep.... I am the gate; whoever enters through me will be saved. (John 10:7,9)

I have come that they may have life, and have it to the full. (John 10:10)

It was winter, and Jesus was in the temple area walking in Solomon's Colonnade. The Jews gathered around him, saying, "How long will you keep us in suspense? If you are the Christ, tell us plainly." Jesus answered, "I did tell you, but you do not believe." (John 10:22-25)

I and the Father are one. (John 10:30)

I am the resurrection and the life. (John 11:25)

But I, when I am lifted up from the earth, will draw all men to myself. (John 12:32)

Then Jesus cried out, "When a man believes in me, he does not believe in me only, but in the one who sent me. When he looks at me, he sees the one who sent me. I have come into the world as a light, so that no one who believes in me should stay in darkness." (John 12:44-46)

For I did not come to judge the world, but to save it. (John 12:47)

[W]hoever accepts me accepts the one who sent me. (John 13:20)

I am the way and the truth and the life. No one comes to the Father except through me. If you really knew me, you would know my Father as well. From now on, you do know him and have seen him. (John 14:6-7)

Don't you believe that I am in the Father, and that the Father is in me? (John 14:10)

And I will do whatever you ask in my name, so that the Son may bring glory to the Father. You may ask me for anything in my name, and I will do it. (John 14:13-14)

Because I live, you also will live. On that day you will realize that I am in my Father, and you are in me, and I am in you. Whoever has my commands and obeys them, he is the one who loves me. He who loves me will be loved by my Father, and I too will love him and show myself to him. (John 14:19-21)

I am the true vine, and my Father is the gardener. (John 15:1)

I have overcome the world. (John 16:33)

Now this is eternal life: that they may know you, the only true God, and Jesus Christ, whom you have sent. (John 17:3)

I have brought you glory on earth by completing the work you gave me to do. (John 17:4)

Righteous Father, though the world does not know you, I know you, and they know that you have sent me. I have made you known to them, and will continue to make you known in order that the love you have for me may be in them and that I myself may be in them. (John 17:25-26)

Jesus...asked them, "Who is it you want?" "Jesus of Nazareth," they replied. "I am he," Jesus said.... When Jesus said, "I am he," they drew back and fell to the ground. (John 18:4-6)

You are right in saying I am a king. In fact, for this reason I was born, and for this I came into the world, to testify to the truth. Everyone on the side of truth listens to me. (John 18:37)

You would have no power over me if it were not given to you from above. (John 19:11)

You can imagine how Jesus must have rocked the establishment with these words as He claimed not only that He was sent from God, but that He actually was *one with God*. The holy God made flesh, speaking words of truth. Words that may rock your world too.

Room for the Kingdom

Find a quiet place and time to read the following poem aloud. Remembering all that Jesus says about Himself in Scripture, contemplate the meanings of the poet's words and images in your own experience. Do you recognize the ways God has moved in your heart to make it a "fit vessel" for His indwelling?

ROOM

You are too large
to be contained within our hearts;
therefore our hearts must be broken,
their iron retaining bands snapped,
expanded along fault lines,
emitting light through
the shattered façade
of our self-sufficiency and pride.
Those whose hearts have been broken
have enough room for the kingdom to grow,
for Jesus to be fully established,
for the Spirit to fill us with life.
A broken heart has fissures
through which living water can flow;
a broken heart cannot hoard
glory, as can a heart unscathed,
closed off, contained.
That very power

which causes a broken heart to live
overflows its capacity,
and is ever replenished
flowing down from the throne
through the wounds of Christ
into our empty souls.
Then out through our fractured hearts
He flows,
to a dry and desolate world.
To be broken is to become
a fit vessel
for the one who was broken for us,
for one too large
for our hearts, intact,
to embrace.[3]

MOMS SPEAK OUT

Susan M.: I think of a couple of times when I have seen God's holiness, and it is awesome. One time I was out running at five o'clock in the morning. It was pitch black, and I looked up in the sky and saw the stars. And it was as if the Lord was saying, "Look, Susan! Look at the stars. See those? *I made those stars.* Do you get that?" And then it was as if He said, "And I made *you.*" I stopped in the road and stood there crying. It was so overwhelming. *That's* the God who made me, and *that's* the God who loved me. That's what I had been struggling with at that time: If I was the only person on the earth, would Jesus have died? It was as if God's voice, through my looking at the stars, was saying, "Yes, I would have died *just for you.* I did this *just for you.*"

Barb: Learning to communicate with my Lord took a giant leap when I realized that even though His holiness meant He was setting up some high standards for my conduct, His mercy and loving understanding were "working" at the same time, because of Christ's sacrifice. In other words, my disobedience didn't shut the door on our relationship.

Sharon: I could've just cried through the church service last week after the point where the pastor, Dave, spoke of how "all creation stopped and held its breath" while Jesus wrestled with God in the garden the night before His death. Think of the rejoicing in heaven when He "took the cup"! Again this week I was stirred by Dave speaking of the "warrior King" who came to save the world. Again the hope of the baby Jesus coming to be the ultimate sacrifice to overcome the dragon really brought me to the point of a healthy fear of God Almighty. It left me with a longing to approach God but not really being able to understand Him at all. Then the sentence of hope—"It is only through the grace of God through Jesus Christ." What a relief! Praise God for giving us an intimate relationship with His Son so that we can know and experience the Father. Community with the Son, then, brings a union with the Father as well. Thanks be to God!

Barb: I will never be in any circumstance or situation or state of heart where Christ would want me to be out of His presence or He would choose to be out of mine. When I really got that concept and understanding down deep in my heart, I knew that I could communicate with Him about *anything* and *everything*—even *nothing!*

Susan M.: As a family we went to visit the Air Force Academy at Colorado Springs. It had been a long trip, and the kids had been rambunctious and were running around. When we walked into the chapel, everyone stopped. We all gasped because our breath was literally taken away: It was so beautiful, and the light—it was early in the morning—was streaming in through those stained-glass windows, and everything was in beautiful symmetry. It was just gorgeous, and even the children stopped whatever they were doing and were quiet and just looked with reverence. It was a very worshipful experience, to think this was a reflection of what God is. I think in our culture we get very little of that.

Lisa: I've got this plague that is incredibly difficult to shake. How many times do I catch myself telling my daughter, "Just a minute, sweetie. Mommy needs to empty the dishwasher or fold this basket of laundry or…(fill in the blank)." Why do I insist that everything be in its place or look orderly before I can enjoy reading to or playing with my daughter? It transcends my relationship with her. It also affects my view of God. Subconsciously I think I have to have my act together and be in the proper frame of mind before I can communicate with God. Before I know it, a long time transpires before I've connected with Him or have given Him the opportunity to speak to me. There's always something that I feel I need to change about myself before I encounter God. When I come upon Scripture or am reminded that Jesus has made me whole and clean *without* my doing, I'm liberated. At that moment I want nothing more than to bask in God's presence…as disheveled as I am.

Susan C.: God's holiness is a concept I find difficult to grasp. I think it is somewhere on the level of eternity; a truth that is nearly impossible to grasp in the confines of our humanity. However, I do find myself repeatedly impacted by Jesus Christ's sacrifice as I contemplate His death for me and how it makes me holy before God! At Easter there is a rather rugged looking cross displayed prominently in our church. That isn't so noteworthy in and of itself, but it is draped with a sash of purple. Many times I have been brought to tears studying that cross: a rough, wooden, common cross, draped in purple, the color of royalty...the King of kings executed as a common criminal for me. I close my eyes, and I see a Man, His frame shrouded in ribbons of bleeding flesh, His face unrecognizable, His hands and feet impaled, and I think, "God! There is God!" Jesus, fully God, became fully man to see through my eyes, to feel my pain, and to bridge the gap between my hopelessness and God's holiness. It's an awesome thought, and my heart can barely contain my gratitude for such a gift. I am holy because of Jesus Christ.

Final Words

I would like to leave you with Paul's words to Timothy. As you read them, keep in mind that this is the God who loves you desperately and wants to know you intimately. This is the God who is taking the risk of letting Himself be known and is exposing His heart and thoughts to you. This is the God who delights in you:

> God, the blessed and only Ruler,
>> the King of kings and Lord of lords,
> who alone is immortal
>> and who lives in unapproachable light,
> whom no one has seen or can see.
> To him be honor and might forever.
>> Amen. (1 Timothy 6:15-16)

May it be so. Through Jesus.
In your life, and mine.

Recommended Reading and Resources

I recommend the following resources, including books and Web sites, for further insight into each of the topics discussed in *The Contemplative Mom*.

CHAPTER 1—OUR RICHEST RELATIONSHIP

Desiring God: Meditations of a Christian Hedonist by John Piper. Sisters, Oreg.: Questar, 1996.

The Family Manager by Kathy Peel. Nashville, Tenn.: Word, 1996.

Finding God by Larry Crabb. Grand Rapids: Zondervan, 1995.

The Imitation of Christ by Thomas à Kempis. New York: Dorset, 1986.

Invitation to a Journey: A Road Map for Spiritual Formation by M. Robert Mulholland Jr. Downers Grove, Ill.: InterVarsity, 1993.

The Jesus I Never Knew by Philip Yancey. Grand Rapids: Zondervan, 1995.

Life and Holiness by Thomas Merton. New York: Image, 1995.

Margin: Restoring Emotional, Physical, Financial, and Time Reserves to Overloaded Lives by Richard A. Swenson. Colorado Springs: NavPress, 1995.

The Message: The New Testament, Psalms and Proverbs, edited by Eugene Peterson. Colorado Springs: NavPress, 1998.

My Utmost for His Highest by Oswald Chambers. Westwood, N. J.: Barbour, 1963.

The Sacred Journey: Drawing Closer to the Heart of God by Brent Curtis and John Eldredge. Nashville, Tenn.: Nelson, 1997.

Seeking the Face of God: The Path to a More Intimate Relationship by Gary L. Thomas. Eugene, Oreg.: Harvest House, 1999.

Side-Tracked Home Executives: From Pigpen to Paradise by Pam Young and Peggy Jones. Anderson, Ind.: Warner, 1983.

Chapter 2—Time Alone with the Beloved

Celebration of Discipline by Richard Foster. San Francisco: HarperSanFrancisco, 1978, 1988.

The Genesee Diary: Report from a Trappist Monastery by Henri Nouwen. New York: Image, 1981.

Gift from the Sea, Anne Morrow Lindbergh. New York: Vintage Books, 1978.

The Life You've Always Wanted by John Ortberg. Grand Rapids: Zondervan, 1997.

Quiet Places: A Woman's Guide to Personal Retreat by Jane Rubietta. Minneapolis: Bethany, 1997.

The Spirit of the Disciplines: Understanding How God Changes Lives by Dallas Willard. Addison, Ill.: Harper & Row, 1988.

Time Management Resources

Getting Organized: The Easy Way to Put Your Life in Order by Stephanie Winston. New York: Norton, 1978.

Organize Yourself! by Ronni Eisenberg. New York: Collier Books, Macmillan, 1986.

Stephanie Winston's Best Organizing Tips: Quick, Simple Ways to Get Organized and Get On with Your Life by Stephanie Winston. New York: Simon & Schuster, 1995.

More Hours in My Day by Emilie Barnes. Eugene, Oreg.: Harvest House, 1982.

CHAPTER 3 — DIVINE COMPANIONSHIP

The Book of Common Prayer. New York: Oxford University, 1990.

A Hunger for God: Desiring God through Fasting and Prayer by John Piper. Wheaton, Ill.: Crossway, 1997.

No Greater Love by Mother Teresa, edited by Becky Benenate and Joseph Durepos. Novato, Calif.: New World Library, 1989.

Pilgrim at Tinker Creek by Annie Dillard. New York: Bantam Books, 1974.

The Practice of the Presence of God by Brother Lawrence. New York: Element, reissue edition 2000.

Artwork online: www.barewalls.com (art posters); www.nga.gov (National Gallery of Art, Washington, D.C.);

http://www.mfa.org/home.htm (Museum of Fine Arts, Boston, Mass.); www.biggallery.com (posters), www.art.com.

Dover Books has inexpensive art postcards and books. Write for a catalog (no Web site or phone orders available): Dover Publications, Inc., 31 East 2nd Street, Mineola, NY 11501-3582.

The following site will send you a Christian quote of the day as an e-mail message. Try them at http://www.gospelcom.net/cqod.

Check company for preprinted scripture background: www.promisechecks.com.

CHAPTER 4—TALKING TO GOD

Answering God: The Psalms As Tools for Prayer by Eugene Peterson. San Francisco: HarperSanFrancisco, 1991.

The Cloud of Unknowing edited by William Johnston. New York: Image, 1973.

Contemplative Prayer by Thomas Merton. New York: Image, 1971.

Meditative Prayer: Entering God's Presence by Richard Peace. Colorado Springs: NavPress, 1996.

Prayer by O. Hallesby. Minneapolis: Augsburg, 1994.

The Way of the Heart by Henri Nouwen. New York: Ballantine, 1991.

Too Busy Not to Pray by Bill Hybels. Downers Grove, Ill.: InterVarsity, 1998.

What Happens When Women Pray by Evelyn Christenson. Colorado Springs: Victor, 1992.

Blank Book/Journal Resources

- Levenger catalog (www.levenger.com) for high-end, acid-free blank books, many of which are leather bound.

- Museum shops or on-line museum stores offer blank books with artwork that are affordable and nourish the visually starved among us at the same time.

- Bookstores such as Barnes & Noble and Borders carry walls of blank books to choose from, or you can order blank books from Amazon.com.

- Stores such as Wal-Mart have inexpensive blank books with and without lines, spiral-bound school-style books (you can look for Snoopy, Bugs Bunny, kittens, and superheroes to lighten things up), or composition books.

- Try a stationery story or office supply store for a neutral, professional look. Here you may find blank pages that match your calendar and planner so you have to carry only one book.

- Make a blank book of your own with a three-hole punch and typing paper, decorating the cover however you wish. I once decorated the cover of my journal with a montage of photos that I covered with contact paper.

- Consider acid-free products, which are available nearly everywhere, though you might try craft stores or Wal-Mart type stores to keep costs lower. By using these, your journals will be around much longer without turning yellow and dog-eared.

- Type "journal" and "journaling" into a search engine, and see what the Internet brings up. I found a few secular sites with helpful ideas.

Chapter 5—Listening to God

Contemplative Bible Reading: Experiencing God Through Scripture by Richard Peace. Colorado Springs: NavPress, 1998.

Hearing God: Developing a Conversational Relationship with God by Dallas Willard. Downers Grove, Ill.: InterVarsity, 1999.

Hind's Feet on High Places by Hannah Hurnard. Uhrichsville, Ohio: Barbour, 1998.

How to Read the Bible for All It's Worth by Gordon D. Fee and Douglas Stuart. Grand Rapids: Zondervan, 1993.

How to Study the Bible for Yourself by Tim LaHaye. Eugene, Oreg.: Harvest House, 1998.

How to Understand Your Bible by John Job and T. Norton Sterrett. Downers Grove, Ill.: InterVarsity, 1982.

Letters Dropt From God by Ruth Vaughn. Kansas City, Mo.: Beacon Hill, 1994.

Lord, Change Me by Evelyn Christenson. Wheaton, Ill.: Victor, 1994.

The Reflective Life by Ken Gire. Colorado Springs: Victor, 1998.

The Return of the Prodigal Son by Henri Nouwen. New York: Image, 1994.

Too Deep for Words: Rediscovering Lectio Divina by Thelma Hall. New York: Paulist, 1988.

A Tree Full of Angels: Seeing the Holy in the Ordinary by Macrina Wiederkehr. San Francisco: HarperSanFrancisco, 1988.

CHAPTER 6—TAKING HIS ADVICE

Abide in Christ by Andrew Murray. Fort Washington, Pa.: Christian Literature Crusade, 1997.

CHAPTER 7—EXPLORING THE GREAT OUTDOORS

The Lessons of St. Francis by John Michael Talbot with Steve Rabey. New York: Dutton, 1997.

My Family and Other Animals by Gerald Durrell. New York: Viking, 1979.

Nature Journaling: Learning to Observe and Connect with the World Around You by Clare Walker, Leslie Roth, and Charles E. Roth. Pownal, Vt.: Storey Books, 1998.

The Original Home Schooling Series, Home Education: Training and Educating Children Under Nine by Charlotte Mason. 1935. Reprint, Wheaton, Ill.: Tyndale, 1993.

Pilgrim at Tinker Creek by Annie Dillard. New York: Bantam Books, 1974.

The Shelter of Each Other: Rebuilding Our Families by Mary Pipher. New York: Ballantine Books, 1996.

"Trees" by Joyce Kilmer, in *One Hundred and One Famous Poems* compiled by Roy J. Cook. Chicago: Reilly & Lee, 1958.

CHAPTER 8—EXPERIENCING COMMUNITY

Church: Why Bother? My Personal Pilgrimage by Philip Yancey. Grand Rapids: Zondervan, 1998.

Going It Alone: Meeting the Challenges of Being a Single Mom by Michele Howe. Peabody, Mass.: Hendrickson, 1999.

The Key to Your Child's Heart by Gary Smalley. Nashville, Tenn.: Word, 1992.

Life Together by Dietrich Bonhoeffer. San Francisco: HarperSanFrancisco, 1954.

Listening for Heaven's Sake: Building Healthy Relationships with God, Self and Others by Anne Clippard, David W. Ping, and Gary R. Sweeten. Cincinnati: Equipping Ministries, International, 1993.

Re-evaluating Your Commitments: How to Strengthen the Permanent and Reassess the Temporary by Maxine Hancock. Minneapolis: Bethany, 1990.

The Safest Place on Earth: Where People Connect and Are Forever Changed by Larry Crabb. Nashville, Tenn.: Word, 1999.

The Shelter of Each Other: Rebuilding Our Families by Mary Pipher. New York: Ballantine Books, 1996.

Marriage-Specific Books and Resources

Give and Take: The Secret to Marital Compatibility by Willard F. Harley Jr. Grand Rapids: Revell, 1996.

The Heart of Commitment by Scott Stanley. Nashville, Tenn.: Nelson, 1998.

His Needs, Her Needs, by Willard F. Harley Jr. Grand Rapids: Revell, 1988.

Intended for Pleasure by Ed Wheat, M.D., and Gaye Wheat. Grand Rapids: Revell, 1997.

The Language of Love by Gary Smalley and John Trent. New York: Pocket Books, 1995.

A Lasting Promise: A Christian Guide to Fighting for Your Marriage by Scott Stanley, Daniel W. Trathen, and B. Milton Bryan. San Francisco: Jossey-Bass Publishers, 1998.

Love for a Lifetime: Building a Marriage That Will Go the Distance by James Dobson. Sisters, Oreg.: Multnomah, 1998.

The Marriage Builder: A Blueprint for Couples and Counselors by Larry Crabb. Grand Rapids: Zondervan, 1992.

Men and Women: Enjoying the Difference by Larry Crabb. Grand Rapids: Zondervan, 1993.

Quiet Times for Couples: A Daily Devotional by H. Norman Wright. Eugene, Oreg.: Harvest House, 1990.

The Family Life Ministries and the Family Life Marriage Conferences: 1-800-FL-TODAY (www.familylife.com).

CHAPTER 9—A LOVE LIKE NO OTHER

The Cost of Discipleship by Dietrich Bonhoeffer. New York: Simon & Schuster, 1995.

The Divine Conspiracy by Dallas Willard. San Francisco: HarperSanFrancisco, 1998.

God Came Near by Max Lucado. Portland, Oreg.: Multnomah, 1987.

The Holiness of God by R. C. Sproul. Wheaton, Ill.: Tyndale, 1998.

The Knowledge of the Holy by A. W. Tozer. San Francisco: HarperSan-Francisco, 1961.

What's So Amazing About Grace? by Philip Yancey. Grand Rapids: Zondervan, 1997.

Your God Is Too Small by J. B. Phillips. New York: MacMillan, 1997.

ACKNOWLEDGMENTS

1. Kelly Monroe, ed. *Finding God at Harvard* (Grand Rapids: Zondervan, 1997).

CHAPTER 1: OUR RICHEST RELATIONSHIP

1. Phillips Brooks, *Sermons* (New York: E. P. Dutton, 1878), on the Christian Quotation of the Day Web site @ http://www.gospelcom.net/cqod/index-05-28-99.html.

CHAPTER 3: DIVINE COMPANIONSHIP

1. Annie Dillard, *Pilgrim at Tinker Creek* (New York: Bantam Books, 1974), 15-6.

2. Ruth Vaughn, *Letters Dropt from God* (Kansas City, Mo.: Beacon Hill, 1994), 17, italics Vaughn's.

3. Mother Teresa, *No Greater Love,* ed., Becky Benenate and Joseph Durepos (Novato, Calif.: New World Library, 1989), 69,71.

4. Mother Teresa, *No Greater Love,* 87.

5. The poem "The Divine Office of the Kitchen" or "Kitchen Prayer" is found on multiple sites on the Internet, but no one seems able to confirm the author's name. Portions of it are often attributed to Brother Lawrence, although a number of variations of the poem exist as an anonymous work. So while I've searched unsuccessfully for the source of this poem, I am grateful to whoever captured the joy and promise of God's divine companionship in the midst of a busy household.

CHAPTER 5: LISTENING TO GOD

1. Chris Rice, "Missing You," *Past the Edges,* BMG Songs, Inc., 1998 (ASCAP).

2. Macrina Wiederkehr, *A Tree Full of Angels: Seeing the Holy in the Ordinary* (San Francisco: HarperSanFrancisco, 1988), 52.

3. Richard Peace, *Contemplative Bible Reading: Experiencing God Through Scripture* (Colorado Springs: NavPress, 1998), 12-3.

4. Peace, *Contemplative Bible Reading*, 101-2.

CHAPTER 7: EXPLORING THE GREAT OUTDOORS

1. John Michael Talbot with Steve Rabey, *The Lessons of St. Francis* (New York: Dutton, 1997), 181.

2. Talbot, *The Lessons of St. Francis*.

3. "Trees," by Joyce Kilmer, in *One Hundred and One Famous Poems*, comp., Roy J. Cook (Chicago: Reilly & Lee, 1958), 39.

4. Mary Pipher, *The Shelter of Each Other: Rebuilding Our Families* (New York: Ballantine Books, 1996), 59.

5. Charlotte Mason, *Home Education: Training and Educating Children Under Nine* (1935; reprint, Wheaton, Ill.: Tyndale, 1993), 79-80.

CHAPTER 8: EXPERIENCING COMMUNITY

1. Quoted in Philip Yancey, *Church: Why Bother? My Personal Pilgrimage* (Grand Rapids: Zondervan, 1998), 37.

2. Mother Teresa, *No Greater Love*, ed. Becky Benenate and Joseph Durepos (Novato, Calif.: New World Library, 1989), 121.

3. Maxine Hancock, *Re-evaluating Your Commitments: How to Strengthen the Permanent and Reassess the Temporary* (Minneapolis: Bethany, 1990), 86.

CHAPTER 9: A LOVE LIKE NO OTHER

1. A. W. Tozer, *The Knowledge of the Holy* (San Francisco: HarperSanFrancisco, 1961), 111.

2. Tozer, *The Knowledge of the Holy*, 112.

3. "Room" by Barbara H. Knuckles, 1998. Used by permission.

About the Author

Ann Kroeker lives in a northern suburb of Indianapolis with her husband, Philippe, and daughters, Isabelle, Sophie, and Nathalie (ages 6, 4, and 2). Kroeker's past writing experience includes several articles that have appeared in magazines such as *Decision, The Student,* and *The Lookout.* She has worked as a correspondent for the *Indianapolis Star* newspaper and *Indianapolis Woman* magazine and as a corporate writer, creating media campaigns and public relations material. She has written and directed hundreds of drama sketches for contemporary churches and assisted the research and writing of *Tough Questions,* a series of seeker small-group study guides written by Garry Poole and Judson Poling for Willow Creek Community Church. When she isn't responding to the frequent call of "Mama," Kroeker applies many of the principles presented in this book to restore her own rich relationship with God.